Contested Mindscapes

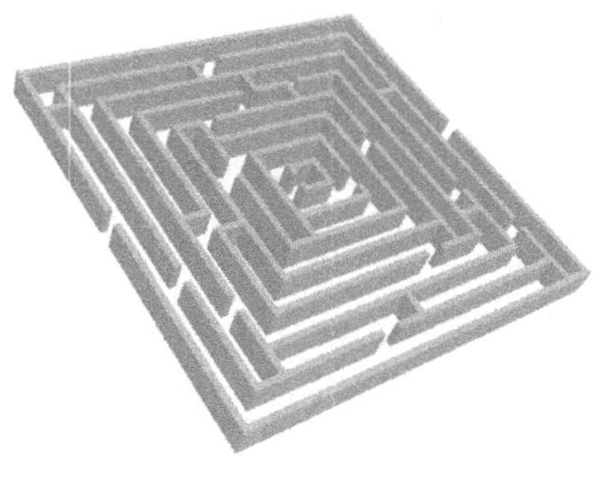

Thomas A. Christie

Other Books by Thomas A. Christie

Liv Tyler: Star in Ascendance

The Cinema of Richard Linklater

John Hughes and Eighties Cinema

Ferris Bueller's Day Off: The Pocket Movie Guide

The Christmas Movie Book

Notional Identities

The Shadow in the Gallery

The James Bond Movies of the 1980s

Mel Brooks: Genius and Loving It!

The Spectrum of Adventure

A Righteously Awesome Eighties Christmas

CONTESTED MINDSCAPES

Exploring Approaches to Dementia in Modern Popular Culture

Thomas A. Christie

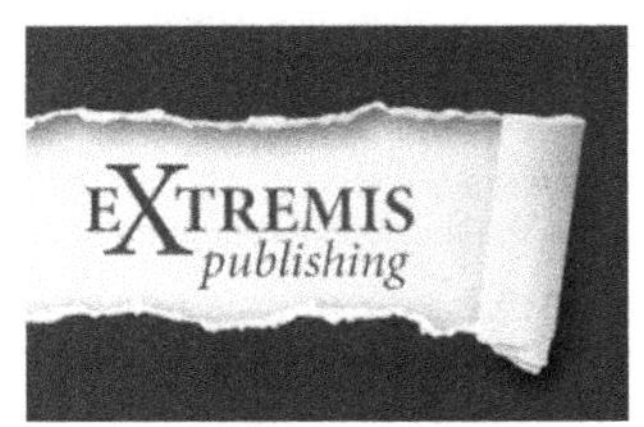

Contested Mindscapes: Exploring Approaches to Dementia in Modern Popular Culture by Thomas A. Christie.

First published in Great Britain in 2018 by Extremis Publishing Ltd.,
Suite 218, Castle House, 1 Baker Street, Stirling, FK8 1AL, United Kingdom.
www.extremispublishing.com

Extremis Publishing is a Private Limited Company registered in Scotland (SC509983) whose Registered Office is Suite 218, Castle House, 1 Baker Street, Stirling, FK8 1AL, United Kingdom.

A CIP catalogue record for this book is available from the British Library.

ISBN: 978-0-9955897-5-9

Typeset in Goudy Bookletter 1911, designed by The League of Moveable Type.

Printed and bound in Great Britain by IngramSpark, Chapter House, Pitfield, Kiln Farm, Milton Keynes, MK11 3LW, United Kingdom.

This book is dedicated to
the loving memory of my
dear and much-missed friend

Mrs Stella Hardwick
(1936-2017)

A long-time advocate of
dementia care, research and support.

Contents

Dramatic and Performance Arts

Video Games and Interactive Entertainment

CONTESTED MINDSCAPES

Exploring Approaches to Dementia in Modern Popular Culture

Introduction

DEMENTIA is a condition which changes lives. According to Alzheimer's Society figures, around 850,000 people in the UK have been diagnosed with the condition at time of writing, with over 42,000 being under the age of 65. The worldwide figure of people affected by dementia is believed to be in excess of 47,000,000, and this overall number is expected to increase sharply in the coming years.

Dementia can take many different forms. Although Alzheimer's Disease is the most commonly-known cause of dementia, other variants can include vascular dementia, dementia with Lewy bodies, frontotemporal dementia, mixed dementia, and numerous other forms of the condition which occur less commonly. Symptoms can include memory loss, language difficulties, issues with orientation, problems with planning and concentration, and complications with visual and spatial skills. Mood swings, delusions and hallucinations may occur as the dementia progresses, with the possibility of challenging behaviours developing over time. The emergence of other symptoms is also possible, depending upon the specific type of the condition that has been diagnosed. Although there is currently no known cure for dementia, support can include medication prescribed to slow its progression, cognitive behavioural therapy, talking therapies, and cognitive stimulation therapy.

Like many forms of mental health disorder, dementia has been wrongly treated as a taboo subject for many years, with the result that the condition is often poorly understood in mainstream culture due to a stubborn reluctance in many quarters to engage frankly with the disorder and its implications. Only within the past few decades have inhibitions surrounding the exploration of dementia been challenged by mainstream popular culture, with the condition now rightly being made the central subject of major creative works as never before.

I am neither a doctor of medicine nor a scientific researcher, and this book is not an examination of the medical realism inherent in portrayals of dementia across nodes of popular culture. It is, however, a project which has personal resonance for me. In the past I have worked at local level for the Alzheimer's Society, and saw for myself the impact of dementia on individual lives. Years later, I worked in an associate capacity with a dementia research unit, investigating the numerous ways in which the condition was being portrayed throughout various nodes of popular culture. Whenever I have worked directly with people who are affected by dementia – either someone who has received a diagnosis themselves, or the people who are close to them – it has always been very apparent to me how much it meant to them to know that they were not alone in what they were facing. Dementia is a condition which has the potential to make people feel fearful, uncertain, lonely, and isolated. But through engaging with various categories of popular entertainment, many people I have spoken to felt that they had found comfort in seeing their difficulties being discussed and explored in mainstream modes of creative expression, knowing that the stigma surrounding their illness was being actively confronted and that public perception of the disorder was being improved as a result. This knowledge often ameliorated, to some extent, feelings of personal seclusion and self-consciousness that they may have had regarding their condition, as they became more aware that other people were encountering many of the same difficulties in their own lives.

While award-winning film dramas such as *Iris* (Richard Eyre, 2001) and *The Iron Lady* (Phyllida Lloyd, 2011), and well-received literary fiction including Lisa Genova's *Still Alice* (2007) and Peter May's *The Lewis Man* (2012), have deservedly been the subject of considerable critical analysis over the passing years, depictions of dementia within nodes of popular culture have often been unfairly neglected by commentators. While clearly not exhaustive by any means, this short book is an attempt to take a look at dementia's depiction within some examples of popular culture in the world today, inspired by subject matter which has been drawn primarily from across the past twenty years. The serious issues of fragmented memory, an undependable sense of identity and unreliable powers of recognition have all been explored within the confines of creative work during this period, and by considering examples from disciplines such as film and television, music, dramatic and performance arts, and video games and interactive entertainment the book will describe some of the different ways in which dementia has been represented within pop culture across the world.

Contested Mindscapes is not intended to be a detailed study in and of itself, but rather a creative tour; an observance of artistic works from across many different media modes which have challenged expectations regarding dementia, encouraging the public to examine their attitudes and responses regarding the condition as well as towards those who are affected by it. In so doing, such artistic works have emphasised the importance of considering and supporting the needs of the individual, of confronting clichés and misconceptions regarding dementia, and ensuring that the condition is brought to the forefront of discussion. But perhaps most importantly of all, this new willingness to fully consider dementia and its many implications will hopefully emphasise to people living with the illness that they are not undergoing a solitary experience; that although no two individuals will ever experience dementia in an exactly identical way, others all over the world are facing the same struggles and complications as an everyday part of their own personal existence. While medical scientists labour tirelessly across the globe to isolate the causes of different forms of dementia and work towards finding a cure, anything that inspires mutual support and a sense of community to encourage people who are affected by the disorder can only ever be a positive development.

The arts have an unparalleled capacity to stimulate meaningful thought and to bring people together in the furtherance of a common cause. If this book succeeds in emboldening only one reader to consider dementia and its effects in a different light, then it will have succeeded in its central aim.

Dr Thomas A. Christie
October 2018

Film and TV

1

PATHOS AND THE SITCOM

Keeping Mum and The League of Gentlemen

THE television situation comedy has a long history within British television; for many decades, some of the most iconic TV moments have established themselves in the popular consciousness through this widespread and influential genre. Television nostalgia compilations regularly draw from scenes such as Arthur Lowe's bumptious Home Guard Captain George Mainwaring urging 'Don't tell him, Pike!' to Ian Lavender's gormless Private soldier in *Dad's Army* (1968-77), or David Jason and Nicholas Lyndhurst – as Derek 'Del Boy' Trotter and his brother Rodney – racing through the streets of Peckham dressed as the 1966 versions of DC Comics' Batman and Robin in John Sullivan's *Only Fools and Horses* (1981-2003). Yet from the work of Galton and Simpson to Lloyd and Croft, it is the ability of the sitcom to present incisive social commentary couched within a comedic framework – even by the subtlest of means – which has come to typify this most iconic of television staples.

Written by Geoffrey Atherden and produced by Stephen McCrum, *Keeping Mum* was arguably one of the most controversial BBC situation comedies to be broadcast in the 1990s. A loose remake of *Mother and Son* (1984-94), an Australian TV comedy which had also been created by Atherden, *Keeping Mum* ran for two series from 1997-98 in the UK and centred around the decidedly fraught suburban life of Andrew Beare (Martin Ball), a man on the cusp of middle age who balanced the care of his elderly mother Peggy (Stephanie Cole) with inevitably fruitless attempts to find employment and maintain some semblance of a social life. The series' dark humour largely stemmed from Andrew's doomed efforts to maintain a vestige of normality in his day-to-day routine, which were inevitably thwarted by his mother's constantly erratic behaviour and the haughty disinterest of his snooty brother Richard (David Haig), an aloof, upwardly-mobile health care professional who was always quick to criticise the quality of Peggy's care while simultaneously doing everything in his power to avoid actively involving himself in it (largely due to his deep-seated fear that it may impinge on his own high-flying personal life).

Keeping Mum met with no small amount of criticism at the time of broadcast, emanating from charitable organisations, newspaper journalists and individuals alike. Although the series did not go so far as to directly reference any one form of dementia in an explicit way, Peggy's memory loss and behavioural difficulties (which were usually geared by the script to cause maximum social embarrassment for Andrew) caused many to advance the opinion that mining humorous potential from people affected by a mental disorder was an inappropriate strategy for a mainstream prime-time comedy, and singularly insensitive towards the emotional needs of carers – not least given the mortifying situations that Andrew invariably found himself mired in. The series' particular emphasis on laboured *schadenfreude* made this observation seem all the more stark, especially when compared to David Renwick's similarly dark *One Foot in the Grave* (1990-2000), a BAFTA award-winning situation comedy which enjoyed great popularity throughout the nineties due to its often enigmatically subversive take on the subject of growing older. Renwick's Victor Meldrew, played with sharp but grumpy aplomb by Richard Wilson, was no stranger to controversial scenes; topics as contentious as elder abuse and suicide were explored by the series, even prompting complaints from the public at times, but humour

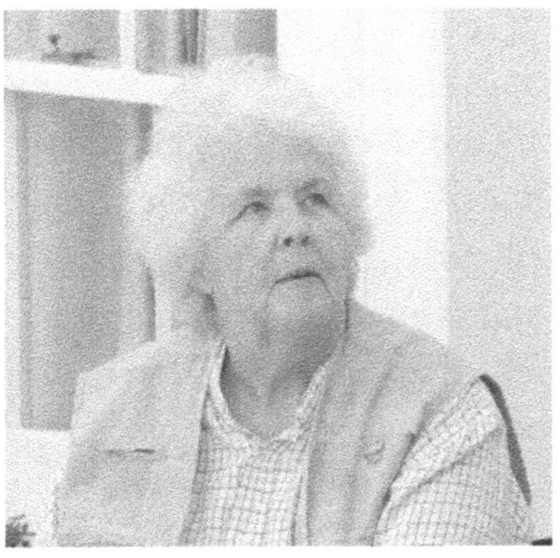

Stephanie Cole

was more often generated by the absurdity of particular situations and the targeting of Victor's curmudgeonly nature than by taking aim at the inevitable pitfalls of progressing ever further into old age.

As Peggy, Stephanie Cole delivered a typically nuanced performance, imbuing the character with brief moments of incisive intelligence and pithy wit just before the character delivers an acutely barbed criticism or some other evidence of inexplicable behaviour, decimating her son's confidence and shredding his nerves in the process. Deliberately playing against the outspoken moral conviction and serrated drollness of her Diana Trent character in Michael Aitkens' earlier, highly successful retirement home-based sitcom *Waiting for God* (1990-94), Cole works hard to lend similar dimension to Peggy as the elderly woman constantly undermines her son's struggle to achieve normality, often single-handedly frustrating everything from his romantic ambitions to his not-unreasonable desire for continuous employment.

Ultimately, however, even a respected veteran actress of Cole's considerable reputation was unable to imbue Peggy with anything approaching a sympathetic aspect; the character inevitably came across as domineering and even slyly manipulative, further irritating those who felt that the programme was trivialising dementia for comedic purposes. The fact that the condition is perpetually obscured by sleight of hand – its symptoms passed off in vague terms of amnesia and volatile behaviour rather than explicitly dealt with as dementia – lends the programme an air of temerity rather than the contemplative treatment it so desperately required, which blunted its effectiveness still further.

This is not to say, however, that *Keeping Mum* was entirely unsuccessful in its creative aspirations. While the series has now all but disappeared from the public consciousness – its short-lived run on the BBC ultimately due to audience indifference rather than a direct result of the sharp criticism which met its broadcast – in more recent years some have questioned whether the series was necessary as thoughtlessly maladroit as it had been portrayed in some corners of the mainstream media. Martin Ball's thoughtful performance as Andrew, for instance, projects just as much care and consideration for his unpredictable mother as it articulates his aggravation at her curious behavioural traits; the motivations of Peggy's actions are often pitched as underhandedly self-centred rather than guilelessly well-meaning but ultimately misguided. He, more than any of the other characters, seems resolved to the fact that it is Peggy's condition, rather than any deliberate attempt on her part to cause hurt or offence, which is the driving force behind the difficulties that she (often inadvertently) causes. Versatile character actor David Haig – so memorable as Major Tom Cadman in Lucy Gannon's military drama *Solider Soldier* (1991-97) and, later, as the twitchy government communications director Steve Fleming in Armando Iannucci's political satire *The Thick of It* (2005-12) – likewise impresses as the self-interested Richard. The series regularly edged closest to conventional comedy when Peggy was pricking the pretentions of her pompous son as he shrewdly (and, often, not so shrewdly) attempted to distance himself from her; though he was to suffer from his mother's acidic put-downs in a manner which suggested some parity with her treatment of Andrew, in actuality her responses made clear her awareness of the unspoken conflict which lay behind the fractious fraternal relationship. That Andrew is willing to sacrifice both professional advancement and social freedom because of a sense of familial duty is not entirely lost on Peggy; her understated discernment of Richard's desire to pay only lip service to his responsibilities, while he seeks to avoid doing anything to tangibly support her, was one of the most insightful aspects of the series.

Paradoxically, however, *Keeping Mum* suffered most from its strangely coy lack of willingness to confront the complex difficulties of dementia head-on – a somewhat ironic situation, given the disapproval that it received on account of the perception that it was making light of the disorder to generate laughs. With Cole's obvious determination to avoid a stereotypical portrayal of an individual struggling with the onset of dementia (even if this meant grappling against the material she was given), and the pathos of Ball's empathetic performance, a more multifaceted approach had the potential to produce a genuinely thought-provoking and compassionate comedy, and there was little doubt that Atherden had ambition to explore the confines of situation comedy in order to use the genre to emphasise some serious points in a seemingly light-hearted way. Sadly, *Keeping Mum* fell some way short of this goal, and its reputation has paled in comparison to the earlier, long-running *Mother and Son*. Content to focus somewhat lethargically upon dementia as a vehicle for the humour of discomfort rather than exploring the series' ability to produce a more subtly-refined exploration of mental health in modern society, *Keeping Mum* had undeniable aspirations to tackle difficult questions about the effects of dementia on family life, but seemed to pull its punches when it came to the sheer complexity of emotion which was involved in such rarefied circumstances.

Some two decades after the divisive premiere of *Keeping Mum*, the BBC would be host to an entirely different approach to dementia within a situation comedy setting – and one which was to reach an entirely different audience. *The League of Gentlemen* was a ground-breaking and genre-defying comedy series which first appeared on BBC Radio in 1997 before making the jump to television between 1999 and 2002. The result would be both successful and influential, having an immediate impact upon popular culture and making stars of the series' ensemble cast. Based (for the most part) in and around the fictional town of Royston Vasey, based in a never-to-be-determined region of the North of England, *The League of Gentlemen* was conceived and written by the creative team of Jeremy Dyson, Mark Gatiss, Steve Pemberton and Reece Shearsmith, with the latter three members appearing in the vast majority of the programme's various roles. Noted for its outlandish characters and deviously plotted storylines, the series exhibited considerable narrative flexibility which ranged from a conventional episodic format in the early years through to an anthology-style Christmas special in 2000, and a complex overlapping plot which weaved throughout the third series in 2002.

The characters who populated Royston Vasey ranged from the obsessively provincial husband-and-wife/brother-and-sister team Tubbs and Edward Tattsyrup, the mysteriously sinister (and possibly supernatural) showman Papa Lazarou, and profoundly unlucky local veterinarian Matthew Chinnery. Among the series' standout figures, however, was Pauline Campbell-Jones (Steve Pemberton), the fanatically bureaucratic Restart Officer at the town's local Job Centre who had monumental contempt for the various jobseekers that she was supposedly tasked with helping find work. Imperious, condescending and exhibiting a bewildering obsession with pens, Pauline eventually became one of the series' most intricately-depicted characters due to a complicated personal journey which saw her losing her job (thus ensuring that she too must become a jobseeker, and suffering as a result of her earlier vainglorious attitudes), and then mounting a desperate but failed attempt to be reappointed to her old post. She is eventually imprisoned as a result of her increasingly extreme efforts to return to employment, and later marries the dim-witted Mickey (Mark Gatiss), a likeable jobseeker who she had once declared unemployable but who (ironically) proves himself able to find work while she remains jobless.

The success of *The League of Gentlemen* led to a number of live performance spin-offs as well as a film,

The League of Gentlemen's Apocalypse (Steve Bendelack, 2005), which ostensibly seemed to bring the story of Royston Vasey to a close by way of a typically postmodern, metafictional strategy. The various members of the team went on to work on numerous other high-profile BBC projects in the intervening years, including *Psychoville* (2009-11), *Sherlock* (2010-) and *Inside No.9* (2014-), but to the surprise of their fans it was announced that they were to temporarily reform in order to produce a special triptych of half-hour episodes to mark the occasion of the twentieth anniversary of the original radio show's broadcast. These episodes were shown on BBC2 in December 2017.

The anniversary specials collectively explored the theme of nostalgia, and most especially the fruitlessness of trying to successfully recreate a past golden age – which may or may not have ever existed in the first place – in a largely indifferent present. To this end, much satire is lavished on the then-recent referendum over Britain's departure from the European Union, with the arch-traditionalist Edward Tattsyrup proudly declaring 'a local country for local people', even as the town of Royston Vasey fights for its very survival as a result of cost-cutting boundary changes. Elsewhere, obsessive toad collector Harvey Denton (Pemberton) – who has died since the events of the original series – is resurrected by his family by means of an arcane ritual which implants his conscious mind into the body of his nephew Benjamin (Reece Shearsmith), only for them to quickly discover that their fond memories of the creepy eccentric were both rose-tinted and gravely misplaced.

However, perhaps the most extreme change amongst the major characters can be found in the formidable Pauline. Once again introduced in a Job Centre setting, the initial scene which re-establishes her to the audience left viewers puzzled due to the fact that the characters appeared to be exactly re-enacting the events of their first appearance back in the first series. It soon becomes clear, however, that all is not as it seems. While Pauline may have appeared as overbearing and authoritarian as always, we become aware that her now-husband Mickey and arch-nemesis, government inspector Ross Gaines (Shearsmith), are among her current cohort of jobseekers – just as they were almost two decades previously. Pauline's familiar ritual of patronising humiliation towards the group of employment hunters is re-enacted, and then abruptly falters. She wanders away from the room, seeming confused and hopelessly lost, when the full scenario is finally revealed. The 'Job Centre' is actually a painstaking recreation that has been set up within a care home, and Pauline is struggling to cope with the symptoms of early-onset dementia.

Mickey, eager to take any course of action that will aid in stimulating Pauline's ailing memory, has arranged for the Royston Vasey jobseekers of the late nineties to attend the 'class' in the hope that it will somehow revive the experiences of Pauline's professional past – and indeed, we see that a trace of her old spark remains when her trademark assertiveness momentarily comes flooding back to the forefront. Yet the creative team's choice of Pauline as the character who is affected by dementia seems acutely deliberate; of all the surreal figures who populate Royston Vasey, she was among the most officious and unbending, her behaviour circumscribed by bureaucratic box-ticking and avowing her sense of primacy over colleagues and jobseekers alike. With that sense of certitude now stripped from her, she appears impossibly adrift in a world of uncertainty and relativity, unable to cling on to the rigid convictions that had for so long defined her thought processes and way of life.

Pauline later meets a tragic end (off-camera) as the result of mistaken identity – a botched contract killing at the hands of the borderline-psychotic Geoff Tipps (Shearsmith), who accidentally invades the wrong house and ends up murdering Pauline instead of his intended target. Mickey is utterly distraught when he later discovers the body of his wife, but the scene is lent additional poignancy by the fact that his well-meaning attempts to help his ailing spouse make the most of her life in defiance of her dementia diagnosis have now reached a heartrending and untimely conclusion due to Geoff's homicidal actions.

Pauline's mental decline is but one part of the anniversary miniseries' overarching theme of the futility of grasping for a bygone past. We can commend Mickey's unstinting efforts to help Pauline try to regain her memories and her old self – even bearing in mind the habitually hostile, tyrannical nature of her pre-dementia state –

and yet we can also see that the success of his labours is limited, and that her deterioration appears to be gathering pace rather than reaching a plateau. It is but one element of a trio of episodes that unsentimentally depicted thwarted hopes and the hidden dangers of wistful reminiscence; self-important, middle-aged community theatre performer Ollie Plimsolls (Shearsmith) daydreams of finding fame as a thespian, only to grudgingly admit that any expectation of critical success has faded with his youth (he is now an ineffectual drama teacher, treated with utter contempt by his students), while warring married couple Charlie and Stella Hull (Pemberton and Shearsmith) have at last divorced and found new partners, only to realise that their lives are actually less happy and fulfilling as a result of having finally moved on from one another; it is as though their personal conflict had come to define them, and without it they are both somehow diminished. And so it becomes clear that while some of these familiar characters are fighting for a brighter but implausibly optimistic future, others are simply content to struggle in order to maintain an increasingly fragile present. Ultimately, all are shown to be disappointed in one way or another.

The main plotline of the anniversary specials, which was the apparent merging of Royston Vasey with a nearby town and the eventual reversal of that decision by the Prime Minister, riffed not-so-subtly on the issue of the Brexit negotiations that were ongoing at the time; Edward Tattsyrup's mouthing of grandiloquent but essentially hollow quasi-nationalistic slogans called to mind the phenomenon of 'cultural dementia' (a term discussed in detail by David Andress in his 2018 book of the same name) and the foggy remembrance of a kind of imperial grandeur that had never truly existed in the form that the unrelentingly provincial Edward seems to suppose. Thus an insightful parallel is drawn between the collective remembrance of an unreachable and/or non-existent bygone age which is impossible to replicate, and Pauline's personal struggle to reconnect with her own past – an effort which becomes all the more poignant for its depiction of those close to her attempting to aid in the reconstruction of a self which is imperfectly filtered through their own unreliable perceptions, in a world which is itself constantly shifting and adapting to meet rapidly-changing needs.

As the anniversary specials draw to a close, Benjamin Denton (Shearsmith) – an occasional visitor to the town – reflects that while we can always revisit old memories, we can never truly relive them in quite the same way as we recall them. The observation perfectly summed up much of the underlying subtext of the mini-series, namely the inevitability of change and the dangers of lionising a wistful longing for the past, but it also provided a pensively melancholic coda to a series that had always sought to push the envelope and provide thoughtful deliberation amongst bouts of uncomfortable laughter. Comparing Pauline's troubled sense of dislocation to the knockabout capers and verbal confusion of Peggy in *Keeping Mum* was to truly emphasise just how far the situation comedy had come in dealing with multi-layered and contentious issues over the past twenty years, demonstrating in no uncertain terms that the format had matured and evolved considerably in that time. Just like the town of Royston Vasey and its denizens, there never really was a golden age of television; only programming that respective viewers had found themselves relating to at specific times of their own personal development, meaning that sentimentality towards the past inevitably means different things to different people. But in its sensitive, far-reaching treatment of dementia – and numerous other controversial topics besides – *The League of Gentlemen* anniversary specials proved that the sitcom has come of age, and has revealed an ability to explore these issues in meaningful and often surprisingly intricate ways.

2

TIME AND INTER-GENERATIONAL RELATIONSHIPS

John Williams' Firefly Dreams

DEMENTIA is a condition which has the potential to have an impact on everyone, no matter their location. It can affect any individual, regardless of their background, social class, gender, sexuality, or nationality. Thanks to the tireless efforts of campaigners, the message of dementia's universal reach is echoing around the world as never before, not least due to the greater awareness made possible via the mass-media and the Internet. One effect of this heightened perception of the condition has been an increased willingness amongst filmmakers to engage with dementia as a central topic of their cinematic works, and certainly many commentators have acknowledged that scrutiny of the topic has become more prevalent since the turn of the century. While several films produced in Europe and the United States have examined the ramifications of dementia – on the lives of those directly affected by it, as well as their friends, their family and their carers – in recent years the subject has also been explored with far greater regularity in cinema originating on other continents.

Writer-director John Williams's award-winning drama *Firefly Dreams* (*Ichiban utsukushi natsu*) (2001) has been praised by many reviewers for addressing the issue of dementia in a fresh and emotionally satisfying manner. Though an expatriate Welshman, Williams was born in the English city of St Albans, and yet his cinematic work has been firmly based in Japan, featuring Japanese dialogue with subtitling available for overseas audiences. Having taught English in Tokyo and Nagoya, Williams came to the attention of critics for his contemplative drama *Midnight Spin* (1996), and he would go on to further success by helming films such as absurdist thriller *Starfish Hotel* and Shakespeare-themed fantasy musical *Sado Tempest* (2012). However, in the eyes of many critics, *Firefly Dreams* remains among his most accomplished work for the big screen.

As striking for its visually remarkable juxtaposition of urban and rural Japan as it is for its delicately-articulated character development, the look and feel of *Firefly Dreams* certainly gives the impression of a feature which is a world away from the hurried pace and laboured moral emphasis of many of its Anglo-American contemporaries. Juxtaposing scenes of the bustling, densely-populated metropolis of Nagoya with the sequences shot in the rural towns of Shinshito and Horai in Aichi Province, where most of the narrative unfolds, Williams demonstrates an unerring respect for Japanese culture and customs while simultaneously peeling back the layers of intergenerational difference to find marked similarities between age groups where disparity and conflict had hitherto been suspected.

The film's plot is, on paper, a deceptively simple one. Teenager Naomi (Maho Ukai), who lives in Nagoya with her parents, has become listless and cynical. She has little time for her education, and finds release in the company of shallow acquaintances who seek increasingly frivolous diversions in an attempt to shut out the grinding monotony of everyday life. Naomi's sybaritic ways soon come to an abrupt halt, however, when her parents' profound marital difficulties cause her father (Atsushi Ono) to temporarily relocate her to the countryside while he tries to deal with the domestic fallout of his wife's (Chie Miyajima) abrupt departure.

Now living with largely unknown relatives in a remote rural area, Naomi finds herself feeling hemmed in, unable to lose herself in the streets of the big city and thus feeling suffocated by her sudden loss of anonymity. She discovers that life at her aunt and uncle's country hotel leads to serious culture clash in comparison to the urban existence that she is used to, and considers it difficult to find commonality with her personable cousin Yumi (Etsuko Kimata), who has learning difficulties.

Naomi gradually begins to question many of her long-held attitudes when she is asked to aid in the care of the elderly Mrs Koide (Yoshie Minami), a wistful, meditative woman who is coming to terms with the onset of Alzheimer's Disease. At first, Naomi considers the support of Koide-san to be little more than yet another tedious chore, but soon re-evaluates her assumptions when she discovers that – during sporadic periods of lucidity – the ageing lady is able to reflect upon the wide-ranging effects that the disorder will have on her life, at exactly the same time that Naomi is being forced by her change in circumstances to challenge her own personal languor and contemplate the direction of her future.

As their friendship develops, Naomi discovers that she has more in common with Mrs Koide than she could ever have imagined. This seemingly-innocuous mature figure had once enjoyed fame as a film actress, Naomi discovers to her surprise, and had survived the widespread destruction of the Second World War to live a rich life packed with abundantly fulfilling experiences. Yet even as Naomi is forced to reconsider her initial assessment of Mrs Koide, the older lady similarly senses something of her own younger self in the headstrong and rebellious Naomi. While the effects of dementia have diminished her capacity to communicate the full range of her life experiences due to the gradual fragmentation of her memories, so too does the changing nature of her ability to engage in social interactions mean that she is able to discuss deeply emotional matters more candidly than may perhaps have been the case in the past.

If the plot of *Firefly Dreams* appears to be lacking in incident, nothing could be further from the truth. Certainly it is not a film which is hugely reliant on a great deal of conventional action, with a small cast, an intimate setting, and a stately pace. However, in terms of emotional impact it can certainly claim parity with even the best-known cinematic depictions of dementia. In Mrs Koide, Yoshie Minami crafts a deeply intricate character with a performance which elevates this conflicted figure far beyond the realms of cliché. Minami had previously been a member of the famous Takarazuka Revue – an all-female musical theatre troupe – and had appeared in Akira Kurosawa's thought-provoking drama *Ikiru* (1952), in which an ennui-stricken bureaucrat desperately attempts to find purpose in his life after receiving a diagnosis of terminal cancer. In a very subtle way, it is left to the audience to decide exactly how Mrs Koide is dealing with her diagnosis of dementia; there is deep ambiguity surrounding her internal balance between treating the reality of her situation as a devastating personal development, or simply as one last stage in a complex life that has been experienced to the full. Such is the confidence of Williams's direction, so much is left tantalisingly unsaid, but the end result cannot fail to be psychologically stimulating.

Likewise, in Naomi we see the actress Maho Ukai (sometimes credited simply as 'Maho') fashioning a similarly elaborate character, shifting from the peer pressure and pop culture obsessions of youth to a less stereotyped, far more multifaceted individual; one who becomes gradually more thoughtful as she is forced to face difficult questions about what she wants from life, and what she can realistically expect from the coming years. The screenplay (also by Williams, who additionally was the feature's producer and film editor) is admirably free of sentimentality; Naomi is no saint even as she begins to confront her personal responsibilities as a result of her new emotional maturity, often being tersely short-tempered with her cousin Yumi, and the film does not offer a traditional happy ending tinged with exultant assurances. Like Naomi herself, members of the audience may find themselves wondering whether Naomi's initial rebellious behaviour was at the root of her family's problems, or whether it was instead caused by her personal reaction to her domestic situation. No concrete answers are ever offered. However, what is less ambiguous is the fact that the rural setting Naomi finds herself in has the facility to offer her authentic bonds of friendship and family that seemed absent from her urban existence. Stripped of the superficialities of her big city life, she finds herself with nowhere left to hide, and eventually makes a number of significant discoveries: that her supportive aunt and uncle (Kyoko Kanemoto and Sadayasu Yamakawa) offer her a more stable domestic environment to that which she has become used to at home; that her acquaintances in the city were fair-weather friends at best; and that she is able to discern entirely new familial benefits such as the low-key leniency of Yumi's easy-going grandfather (Haruo Hanahara), who turns a blind eye to her occasional indulgences.

The contrast between youthful exuberance and elderly wisdom has, of course, been employed many times over the course of cinema history, as has the jarring disparity been drawn between impersonal urban landscapes and socially cohesive rural locales. At the time of the film's release, a number of critics drew understandable comparisons between the plot developments of *Firefly Dreams* and those of the Academy Award-winning *On Golden Pond* (Mark Rydell, 1981), which similarly drew upon intergenerational understanding as the engine of its narrative incidents. Yet in truth, Williams managed to provide a refreshing enough angle on his narrative to create an experience which was quite different in execution, allowing his actors ample room to breathe which resulted in a rewarding depth of performance without ever risking the danger of allowing the film to descend into a formula whose over-familiarity would have strained the viewer's patience.

Firefly Dreams is the kind of film which, regrettably, comes along all too rarely. With Yoshinobu Hayano's mesmerising cinematography making the most of a scenic modern-day pastoral Japan that is sadly too often unknown to international audiences, and aided by Paul Rowe's reflective original score, the feature makes full use of a relatively small cast to bring the issue of intergenerational friendship to life in a tenderly-realised way. Yet in its presentation of dementia, Williams's sensitively-composed screenplay and Minami's delicately restrained performance combine to impart a truly memorable evocation of the complicated and comprehensive way that the condition can affect someone's life at any age, though specifically exploring the sense of existential crisis that can arise in later years. We see the fascinating life of a skilled, talented and wise woman as though reflected in the shards of a broken mirror; the experiences of this strong character shine no less brightly for their involuntary deconstruction, and their continued relevance is shown to have value not only to Mrs Koide on a personal level, but also in their power to reshape Naomi's realisation of who she is and what she might yet become.

The film may lack the swift narrative pacing of many Western offerings from the same period, but in turn *Firefly Dreams* offers up a ruminative and genuinely investigative approach to ageing and life choices that are seldom to be witnessed in much of mainstream Western cinema today. Williams presents viewers with a narrative experience of unusual power and subtlety, contrasting the old and young, the urban and rural, the modern and traditional, the highly social and grindingly indifferent. In this attempt to emphasise the collective universality of dementia's effects by such respectful, contemplative and non-exploitative means, to say nothing of its accomplished evocation of a contemporary Japan that is rarely to be appreciated by international audiences, *Firefly Dreams* can only be commended for its ambition.

3

THE MANY FACES OF DEMENTIA

Alan Alda and Portrayals of Mental Health in ER and Diminished Capacity

ALPHONSO D'Abruzzo, better known by his professional name of Alan Alda, is a six-time Emmy Award and Golden Globe Award-winning actor and one of the most celebrated polymaths in American popular culture. As famous as he has become for his performances on stage and screen, he has also worked as a writer and author, director and screenwriter, and – for several decades – as an outspoken advocate for many issues ranging from equal rights in society to the promotion of science. Forever remembered for his eleven-year stint in the role of iconoclastic army surgeon Dr Benjamin Franklin 'Hawkeye' Pierce in CBS's *M*A*S*H* (1972-83), one of the highest rated television shows in history (the final episode drew a staggering 125 million viewers, making it one of the most-watched transmissions of all time), in recent years Alda has won a new generation of admirers thanks to his high-profile recurring appearance as veteran Republican senator and presidential nominee Arnold Vinick in NBC's acclaimed political drama *The West Wing* (1999-2006). In addition to his steadfast furtherance of the arts and humanities throughout his long career, he has also become a prominent advocate for awareness of Parkinson's Disease, announcing in July 2018 that he was himself affected by the condition.

Because of his well-publicised support for scientific and medical research (not least through the establishment of the Alan Alda Center for Communicating Science, founded in 2009, for which his high-profile advocacy was the central inspiration), it comes as little surprise that Alda has engaged with the subject of dementia throughout his prolific and diverse acting career. What is perhaps more remarkable is the fact that the portrayal of the subject which has emerged throughout his various performances has proven to be so intensely polished and multifaceted. As he has revealed in interviews over the years, Alda's own mother was affected by dementia throughout the 1980s in the period following the conclusion of *M*A*S*H*, and his personal experience of the condition has informed his acting approach in a number of interesting ways. As someone who understands both the trauma and the manifold implications of the disorder, Alda's performances reveal two contrasting aspects of dementia: that a diagnosis profoundly alters individual lives, and that life must go on regardless.

Alda's first prominent engagement with a character who is affected by dementia came during the October and November of 1999, during his short but roundly applauded portrayal of Dr Gabriel Lawrence on NBC's long-running medical drama *ER* (1994-2009). Lawrence is the former mentor of series regular Dr Kerry Weaver (Laura Innes), who is involved in her old instructor's appointment as Senior Attending Physician within the series' eponymous Emergency Room. The veteran doctor has had an illustrious career, to say nothing of a hard-won reputation for a high degree of diagnostic capability, so his recruitment is met with widespread approval by the senior practitioners.

But soon it becomes apparent that all is not as it seems where this new medical appointment is concerned. Though witty, intelligent and often avuncular in his manner, Lawrence becomes prone to inexplicable episodes of anger and frustration. His memory falters at random points, causing him to have difficulty remembering words and expressions or forgetting important details. Later, his memory loss becomes more severe; first these lapses seem relatively innocuous, such as when he loses his reading spectacles (later to be recovered from a freezer unit). But as time passes, he is unable even to remember where he has parked his car. Though he is initially resistant to any suggestion that his mental capacity is deteriorating, eventually the diagnosis of the early stages of Alzheimer's Disease proves impossible to evade.

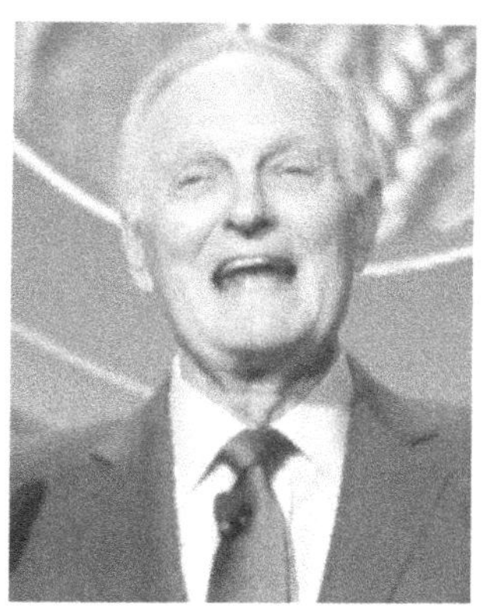
Alan Alda

Alda won much critical praise for his sensitive and believable portrayal of Dr Lawrence, from the character's unpredictable mood swings to his eventual aching sense of helplessness, and his proficiency in the role was to see him nominated for an Emmy Award. The performance won favourable comparisons to his earlier, legendary appearance as Hawkeye Pierce – not just in terms of the Lawrence character's medical background, but also in the revelation of his early years working for the United States Army. Similarly, it was noted that Alda never overplayed the slow-burning but ultimately impotent rage of an intellectual powerhouse who is struggling with the knowledge that his mental abilities are faltering. But what especially stood out for many commentators was the way in which the character was developed beyond simply his utility as a vehicle for exploring issues that were related to dementia. Dr Lawrence was a fully-formed individual with many dimensions, and his often-complex relationships with the other characters was fleshed out fully – along with his emotional response to a failed marriage and the effects of his estrangement from his son (the capricious relationship between them, and subsequent attempts to rectify it, formed a crucial part of the character's story arc). Though Lawrence is forced to cope with the harsh realities of living with dementia – having diagnosed it in others over the years, he now has no choice but to deal with the onset of the condition himself – the regular cast of medical professional characters are able to support him in coming to terms with his eventual resignation from an eminent and long-running career.

His appearance on *ER* had very much been a portrayal of dementia which was dramatic in nature, but Alda was to return to the subject with a different approach some years later in Terry Kinney's cinematic comedy *Diminished Capacity* (2008). Co-starring actors Matthew Broderick and Virginia Madsen, Alda was cast in the role of larger-than-life Rollie Zerbs, a gentleman entering old age who has been diagnosed with Alzheimer's Disease. Because of the challenges posed by the progression of the condition, Rollie's sister is in the process of ensuring his long-term support by seeking to have him admitted to a local nursing home. Rollie, however, considers this move to be an unwelcome constraint on his personal freedom, and hatches a plan to continue living independently. In the possession of a prized 1908 Chicago Cubs baseball card, he enlists the support of an unlikely ally in the form of his nephew – a journalist who is temporarily affected by amnesia following a concussion – and outlines a strategy to travel to Chicago and sell the rare card for the largest amount of money possible, thus enabling him to live at home with the regular support of professional caregivers.

A light-hearted road trip ensues, with Rollie's plan hitting more than a few snags before the film reaches its climax. At times he sporadically forgets the value of the card, leading to unwanted interest from interlopers keen to separate him from it by less-than-legal means, while his nephew Cooper is distracted by the unexpected effects of his own memory loss as well as the sudden appearance of an old flame from his youth. The thrust of the film lies in the touching emotional bond which is struck up between the two men, one struggling with an impaired memory on a short-term basis while the other knows that his mental capacity is continuing to irreversibly decline. For Rollie, dementia is not something to be raged against, but rather a warning that he should make the most of every moment of his life while he can – though his abilities may change as the condition progresses, he seems determined to maintain a positive and constructive outlook for as long as possible. Yet even this aim sometimes proves difficult, for in some of the film's most potently affecting scenes we see the character's sunny disposition briefly penetrated by frustration, anger, desperation, and powerlessness.

Though *Diminished Capacity* did not prove to be as renowned an entry on Alda's filmography as his earlier appearance as Dr Lawrence had been, and certainly was not to be a box-office smash in terms of commercial performance, the film's life-affirming ethos and a screening at the Sundance Film Festival in 2008 won guarded approval from some critics while being greeted with scepticism by others. Yet though some were to give voice to the perennial question of whether dementia can ever be an acceptable subject for a comedy film, Alda proved once again that he would not use the condition as a means to define a character, but rather by delineating it as only one factor – albeit a powerful one – which influences an individual's life at a particular stage. In a commendably layered performance, he brings emotional depth to Rollie's personal journey, never allowing this gregarious, flamboyant character's disorder to be treated glibly or with anything less than appropriate respect.

With Gabriel Lawrence and Rollie Zerbs, Alda had given performances which examined two sides of a life-changing condition; whether in an eminent professional's struggle against mental decline or an amiable eccentric's battle to remain positive and optimistic in the face of the progressive deterioration of his psychological capacity, the viewer is left in no doubt of the serious long-term effects of a dementia diagnosis, and through these roles Alda does not shirk from emphasising the personal impact of the disorder. A human being is never simply the receptacle for a set of symptoms, he demonstrates, but rather a living person who will always have unique qualities and individual needs. Thus he places equal importance on the need to focus upon both the general and the specific; by employing an approach which amalgamates the prominence of the individual with the inescapable progression of the symptoms of dementia, Alda uses Lawrence's emotional reconciliation with his long-lost son and Rollie's spirited attempts at personal liberation to highlight the fact that life can continue to be meaningful and productive even after a diagnosis of the condition has been made. In so doing, he encourages the viewer to celebrate life irrespective of age, background or medical conditions, underscoring the need to strengthen that which unites us rather than bemoaning aspects which have the potential to divide.

Because of Alda's continued high public profile, his performances have done much to bring the effects of dementia to a wide audience, aiding in the much-needed destigmatisation of the condition. His dramatic take on its symptoms in *ER* highlighted the personal impact of the condition rather than diminishing it, whereas the comedy content of *Diminished Capacity* never trivialised the effects of dementia but instead was to accentuate the need for meaningful personal support and greater understanding towards those who are affected by it. Though Alda, for all his many creative accomplishments, may always be fated to be synonymous with the laconic Hawkeye Pierce thanks to his long-running, trailblazing appearance in *M*A*S*H*, it seems clear that the low-key but highly constructive contribution he has made to the understanding of dementia through his choice of roles in later life has been of considerable value to public understanding of the effects of the disorder upon individual lives.

4

LIVING LONG AND PROSPERING

Changing Representations of Dementia in the Star Trek Franchise

IN all its various media, from literature to cinema, science fiction has a proven track record of dealing with hard-hitting issues, often by allegorical or indirect means, and at the forefront of this drive for greater understanding of the human condition for more than five decades has been the stalwart *Star Trek* television franchise. The voyages of the Starship *Enterprise* have, since the 1960s, provided the basis for an exploration of topics ranging from international foreign affairs to social justice. Often neglected, however, is the series' capacity to explore more personal matters such as those deriving from mental health, and to face up to the implications that psychiatric and psychological conditions can present for the individual.

Star Trek's brushes with the issue of dementia have not always been frequent, but given the hundreds of episodes that have been aired between the mid-sixties and the present day, the franchise has never attempted to evade the presentation of a rounded depiction of the condition. At the time of writing, *Star Trek* has undergone something of a renaissance within popular culture as a result of the success of the new CBS All Access series *Star Trek: Discovery* (2017-), involving events set a decade prior to the ground-breaking original series. This new take on the franchise has continued to demonstrate the progressive nature of previous incarnations of the show, with a clear aim of inclusiveness and optimism for the future that its creator, the late Gene Roddenberry, would surely have approved of. Already, in its first season alone, *Discovery* has presented a major recurring character – Lieutenant Ash Tyler (Shazad Latif) – who suffers a breakdown with symptoms similar to those of Post-Traumatic Stress Syndrome when he discovers that he is actually a member of the alien Klingon species. With his true memories suppressed and his original personality submerged beneath a deliberately manufactured persona, Tyler's psychological distress is handled in an admirably uncompromising way, and has proven that new iterations of *Star Trek* continue to treat mental health issues with both respect and sensitivity.

Star Trek's engagement with the issue of dementia started back in 1967 with 'The Deadly Years', an episode from the second season of the original *Star Trek* TV series (1966-69), broadcast on NBC. During a mission to supply essential materials to a distant human colony on planet Gamma Hydra IV, Captain James T. Kirk (William Shatner) and his shipmates are affected by peculiar radiation from the trail of a transitory comet which causes them to age by approximately thirty years for every day that passes. As well as undergoing rapid physical deterioration, the mental wellbeing of the affected crew is also compromised. Kirk, the archetypal quick-thinking man of action, becomes confused and indecisive. Mr Spock (Leonard Nimoy), the half-Vulcan science officer famed for his towering intellect, discovers that he is having memory problems and suffering from severe lethargy.

As Kirk emphasises, his function as a commander is impaired not so much by the fact that his bodily frailties have rendered his usual fast reflexes and swashbuckling capabilities impossible, but rather by the toll that the radiation has had on the acuity of his thought processes. Given to uncharacteristic outbursts and violent fluctuations in mood, his executive functions soon erode to the point that – much to his chagrin – a less experienced officer is eventually forced to supplant his command of the ship.

Dementia presents a kind of professional nightmare for a character like James T. Kirk; a fact that the episode makes with commendable thoughtfulness. The condition first robs him of his trademark cunning and decisiveness, then leads him into the depths of disorientation, and finally undermines his hitherto-unshakeable sense of authority by allowing him to be weakened and eventually usurped by a largely-untested rival (a consequence which, due to the temporary commander's inexperience and disastrous leadership decisions, almost results in the destruction of the ship). Even the episode's resolution, where some out-of-the-box thinking by an ailing Spock and the ship's chief surgeon Dr Leonard McCoy (DeForest Kelley) restores the afflicted crewmembers to their normal health (and correct physical age), helps to underscore the point that it is Kirk's intellectual vitality rather than just his physical fitness which is most essential to the smooth operation of the ship.

Dementia proved to be an antagonist that Kirk and his crewmates only barely manage to defeat; unlike more recognisable *Star Trek* villains such as the Klingons, the condition cannot be reasoned with or outmanoeuvred. This theme of ongoing psychiatric deterioration as an adversary to be fought against would resurface many years later in 1994 with 'All Good Things...', the final episode of sequel series *Star Trek: The Next Generation* (1987-94). Here, Kirk's successor – Captain Jean-Luc Picard (Patrick Stewart) – finds himself trapped in a future reality where he is in the latter stages of the fictional 'Irumodic Syndrome', a form of dementia which exhibited various symptoms including hallucinations, memory loss and intense variations in mood. Unsure of the authenticity of his surroundings, unable to trust the motives of those close to him, and beset by a deep suspicion of what his senses appear to be telling him, Picard finds himself becoming ever more helpless in the face of mounting danger.

More so even than Kirk, Picard is a cerebral figure, far more inclined to puzzle out a winning strategy than to shoot first and ask questions later. His sudden incapability to discern reality from delusion, therefore, proves devastating to someone whose command ability is so closely wedded to his impressive powers of observation and deduction. Through the lens of his Cartesian struggle to distinguish between the real and the unreal, the possible and the probable, the viewer determines a vague taste of the frustration which characterises the corrosive effect that dementia can have on even the most fundamental aspects of perception.

Intriguingly, what was to be arguably *Star Trek: The Next Generation*'s definitive exploration of the condition had actually taken place some years beforehand during the episode 'Sarek' (1990). The eponymous character, legendary Vulcan ambassador Sarek (Mark Lenard), was long established in the series as the father of science officer Spock, and thus his employment in this particular episode lent it considerable emotional impact amongst long-time followers of the series.

Throughout his appearance in the original series, and various encore performances during its spin-off cycle of films, the scholarly Sarek was depicted by respected character actor Lenard as the epitome of logic and intellectualism. During what appears to be a routine diplomatic mission, the elderly ambassador is being transported by the Starship *Enterprise* to his destination when it becomes apparent that all is not as it should be. The ship's crew, highly-trained and professional, begin bursting into inexplicable fits of anger, leading Captain Picard and his officers to suspect that an unexpected cause lies behind these atypical lapses in temper. It eventually emerges – though it is not common knowledge – that Sarek is affected by 'Bendii Syndrome', a fictional form of dementia which affects Vulcans and is characterised by many symptoms that are similar to human dementias, including memory loss and fluctuations in mood. What makes Sarek's condition all the more dangerous is the fact that, as Vulcans are a telepathic species who suppress their emotions, he is unwittingly projecting the violent vacillations in his feelings onto others, and in ways that they can neither predict nor repel. Eventually a crisis is averted when Sarek engages in a 'mind meld' – a technique of joining consciousness between beings, which is unique to Vulcans – with Picard, allowing him to temporarily draw from the famously self-controlled Captain's reserves of discipline and willpower. However, there is no futuristic 'magic bullet' to cure Sarek's affliction in the long-term; his mental deterioration continues as a result of his condition, and the character dies off-screen after making one final brief appearance in the famous two-part episode 'Unification', which aired the following year and returned Leonard Nimoy to televised *Star Trek* for the first time in decades.

The *Star Trek* franchise's other explorations of dementia have generally tended to focus on a central aspect of identifying the difficulties inherent in distinguishing an authentic reality from an illusory environment. *The Next Generation* episode 'Frame of Mind' (1993), for instance, was to see the *Enterprise*'s first officer – Commander William T. Riker (Jonathan Frakes) – being mentally programmed by aliens to believe that he is affected by symptoms similar to those of vascular dementia, plunging him into deep anxiety as he is faced by numerous overlapping variations of reality (or, more precisely, what he perceives to be reality) which contradict and contend with each other. Further confusing his situation is the fact that the mental realities he is facing are linked in unusual ways; he is appearing as the central character in a stage drama which deals with the thin line between materiality and illusion, while simultaneously struggling with adjacent existences where he is preparing to undertake a dangerous mission on an alien planet, and is also a patient within an asylum for criminals with mental health issues who is repeatedly told that he is currently awaiting trial on a murder charge. Just as Riker has no idea who or what to believe, so too are the audience left to deliberate on the true nature of his predicament. Only at the conclusion of the episode, where his mental distress and hallucinations are revealed to be the result of a technological mind probe, does the normally-unflappable first officer come to realise that the fierce

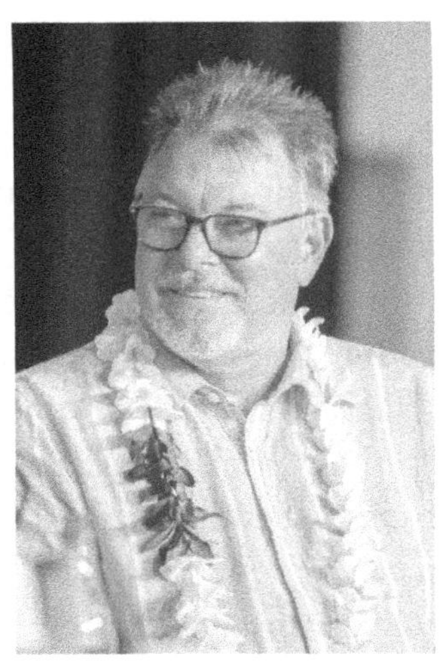

Jonathan Frakes

battle which had raged over the various divergent realities was really a result of his own subconscious mind rebelling against those who were attempting to interrogate it for their own ends (that is, to glean intelligence on the *Enterprise* and the rest of the Starfleet).

Later spin-off series *Star Trek: Voyager* (1995-2001) was similarly to riff on this theme, and often in increasingly innovative ways. 'The Fight' (1999) obliquely dealt with the damage to cognition which derives from dementia pugilistica (now known as chronic traumatic encephalopathy), a neurodegenerative condition which can present itself in people who have experienced multiple head injuries (such as boxers, hence the disease's original name, though it has also been found in athletes competing in a wide range of different contact sports). The condition has become marked by symptoms which may include oscillations in mood, behavioural issues, and cognition problems, and these indicators were explored in 'The Fight' when Commander Chakotay (Robert Beltran), first officer of the Starship *Voyager*, unexpectedly becomes affected by them when the vessel enters a region of the cosmos known as 'chaotic space'.

Following a recreational computer boxing simulation in which he spars with a holographic opponent, Chakotay is knocked out and awakens in the ship's sickbay, complaining of a blinding headache. At first this is assumed to be a result of his boxing match, but after recounting details of a hallucination he had experienced the ship's medical officer – the Doctor (Robert Picardo) – discovers unusual activity in Chakotay's visual cortex.

As the state of delirium becomes more acute, the Doctor eventually deduces that the first officer carries the genetic marker for a cognitive disorder which – though previously dormant – has now suddenly become active, possibly as a result of their location in an area of space where the laws of physics are in perpetual flux. Chakotay is alarmed, not least given his fears that his dementia will progress in the same manner as that of his grandfather's (presumably another carrier of the same genetic marker).

Eventually, after some intensive investigation, the *Voyager*'s commander – Captain Kathryn Janeway (Kate Mulgrew) – and her team of officers realise that chaotic space has somehow altered Chakotay's DNA at a level so precise that auditory and optical neurons have been divested of protein insulation to specifically enable him to receive particular targeted hallucinations. The first officer enters a meditative state, but is continually besieged by visions of a non-existent boxing match. Thus he comes to realise that aliens who exist beyond the corporeal realm are trying to communicate with him, but is reluctant to listen to their message as he is terrified that he will lose his tenuous grip on sanity altogether.

Becoming increasingly irrational and unable to discern between reality and the aliens' realignment of his DNA, Chakotay begins to imagine that he is actually a professional boxer and that the unseen creatures are his opponent. He becomes uncharacteristically violent and unpredictable, but eventually realises that – in spite of appearances – the aliens are not hostile at all, but are actually attempting to warn *Voyager* to leave the area before the ship comes to harm. As they have no way of communicating with the crew via conventional means, their only plan of action is to hijack Chakotay's neurology and pass on their message via his resulting hallucinations. Informing him of a way to recalibrate the ship's sensors to take into account the strange physical laws of chaotic space, the aliens essentially give Chakotay the lifeline that he needs to pull *Voyager* out of danger. Once free of the influence of this strange region, the beleaguered first officer gradually returns to full health.

'The Fight' provided an intriguing premise for utilising dementia-like symptoms within a science fiction plotline in a way which never seemed gratuitous or sensationalist. The climactic boxing match between Chakotay and the illusory 'Kid Chaos', where the aliens finally make their intentions known, was a truly striking sequence which blended hallucinogenic imagery with a disorienting sound environment to produce a highly effective air of genuine delirium. Perhaps more importantly, Chakotay's breakdown is never played solely as a driving factor of plot progression; the tumultuous, unpredictable nature of the external threat is handled believably by the imperturbable, self-disciplined first officer, and by derailing his meditative

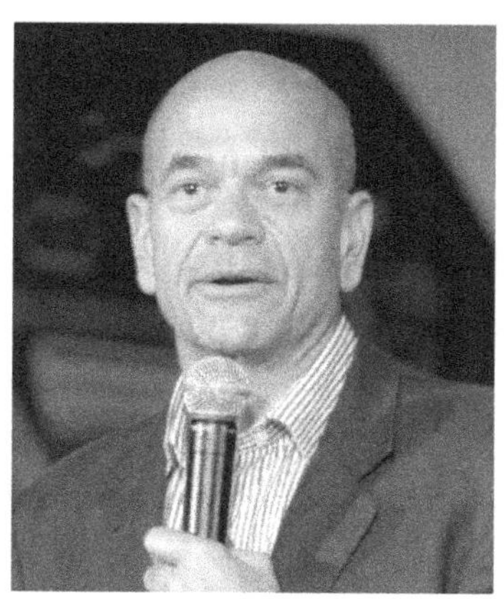

Robert Picardo

'vision quest' we see the usually restrained Chakotay slowly descend into irrationality and mental disarray.

In *Star Trek*, not even computers were immune from the effects of dementia. *Voyager*'s holographic medical officer, the Doctor, was a complex artificial intelligence who found himself at the heart of an existential crisis in one of the series' earliest episodes, 'Projections' (1995). Exploring a computer-based form of dementia entitled 'holo-transference dementia syndrome', we see the Doctor facing the prospect that he is in the throes of a condition which leads an artificial intelligence with the physical form of a human to believe that they are real and that the world around them is merely an illusion. The result was a familiarly Cartesian interpretation of being and perception, though one which was commendable for its ambition by using as its focus a character whose very existence derived from silicon rather than carbon.

Facing a strange situation whereby the ship appears to have been abandoned leaving only him aboard, the Doctor is alarmed when he begins to exhibit physical life signs (thought impossible in a holographic projection) and then discovers that he is in fact Dr Lewis Zimmerman, his original programmer who was responsible for the creation of the hologram's personality and other characteristics. Eventually he is faced with a scenario whereby he appears to be a character in a simulation to analyse the effects of long-term isolation in space, but it soon seems that the program's data has become corrupt. Over time he becomes persuaded that he must destroy the simulated ship in order to free himself from the increasingly malfunctioning reality that he is in, but is stopped at the last moment by Chakotay, who appears out of the blue (and thus abruptly punctures the Doctor's elaborate delusionary state) to dissuade him from this desperate course of action. After subsequently encountering numerous overlapping realities, the Doctor comes to realise that the illusion of him having become his own creator was actually the result of a surge in radiation from a spatial anomaly which had affected his core programming. In essence, his internal psychology had been attempting to make sense of the situation in the only way it could. Though unsure exactly what to believe, even after the crisis is resolved, the Doctor is gradually able to recognise that his 'true' reality is indeed the authentic one, and that he has not been permanently affected as a result of the radiation's effects on the data which determines his character and personality attributes.

Pursuing the basic notion of what reality actually is, and how it may be recognised or quantified, is certainly not a new line of enquiry for a science fiction television franchise such as *Star Trek*. Depictions of dementia, however, are markedly less common, and although the series initially seemed almost apprehensive about discussing the condition explicitly, it should be applauded for having consistently treated the issue in a manner which was serious and never overtly exaggerated for dramatic effect. In exploring the disorder by examining its effects on regular characters in the series, with whom viewers have had the opportunity to establish emotional investment (sometimes over several years), television drama has a unique ability to present sensitive issues such as mental health in an inventive and meaningful way, and the *Star Trek* universe – with its overriding themes of equality, fairness, and social justice – provides the perfect foundation upon which to construct a consequential engagement with a subject which has deep personal relevance for an increasing number of people.

5

DEMENTIA AND THE CHALLENGE OF DEDUCTION

Nicolas Boukhrief's Cortex

DEMENTIA has been a subject with which mainstream cinema has, thus far, had a febrile and relatively uneasy relationship. Dealt with relatively uncommonly by film-makers in past decades, it has only been since the turn of the century that the condition has been explored in greater depth by directors in a manner that can be considered truly international in scale. However, narrative engagement with dementia to date has largely been confined to award-winning biopics such as *The Iron Lady* (Phyllida Lloyd, 2011), or harrowing emotional dramas which have included *Away From Her* (Sarah Polley, 2006) and *Amour* (Michael Haneke, 2012). Only in recent years has the subject started to be tentatively addressed in comedy-dramas and other popular genres of film, a development which has helped to heighten audience awareness of the condition and how it has the potential to affect individuals of any age or background.

One of the most unconventional cinematic explorations of dementia has come in the form of *Cortex*, a film directed by Nicolas Boukhrief which was released in 2008. Produced in France, and featuring French dialogue throughout, *Cortex* is a rare example of the symptoms of dementia being highlighted within the thriller genre – not simply as a plot device, but rather as the central core of the film's narrative. The action features a retired police inspector named Charles Boyer (a mesmerising performance by veteran actor André Dussollier) who, having been diagnosed with dementia at an early stage in its onset, discovers that he is having difficulty living independently. Concerned for his future, Boyer makes the difficult decision to leave his home, relocating to The Residénce – a clinic which specialises in the treatment of neurological conditions. As the inspector settles into life at the institute, he soon becomes increasingly concerned when he learns that other residents are disappearing under mysterious circumstances, supposedly dying from unexplained causes. However, Boyer feels uncertain of how far he can trust his instincts – honed over many years in the police force – as the progressive effects of dementia continue to affect his cognitive abilities. Can he determine the nature of the apparent murders that he is witnessing around him, when he cannot even be sure that any crime has really taken place?

Thanks to Dussollier's fascinatingly charismatic central performance, *Cortex* is a film which will make even die-hard mystery buffs work hard to unravel the conundrum at the heart of the narrative. In spite of its genre trappings, this is no straightforward whodunit. The tightly-written screenplay by Boukhrief and Frédérique Moreau never relies on an exploitative employment of dementia as a simple mechanism of the plot, instead ensuring that the condition is dealt with sensitively and as fundamental to the film's approach. In this sense, Boukhrief echoes the careful construction of a delusional mindset which would prove so pivotal to Martin Scorsese's later adaptation of Dennis Lehane's *Shutter Island* (2010), leaving the audience genuinely uncertain as to how far they can trust the protagonist's perception – to the point that even the character can himself be seen to doubt their own judgement.

At the time of *Cortex*'s release a number of critics were to draw parallels with Christopher Nolan's *Memento* (2000), a perplexing but captivating exploration of amnesia where the effects of memory loss are key to the film's mystery. In truth, however, *Cortex* displays a different and broader range of concerns, unflinchingly addressing issues of the anxieties related to ageing and the apprehension which accompanies the gradual loss of key abilities due to dementia. (The sequence in the Paris Metro in particular emphasises an unnerving range of overlapping emotions in Boyer who, used to the toughest cases of detection, struggles in undisguised frustration to understand a chart showing underground stations.)

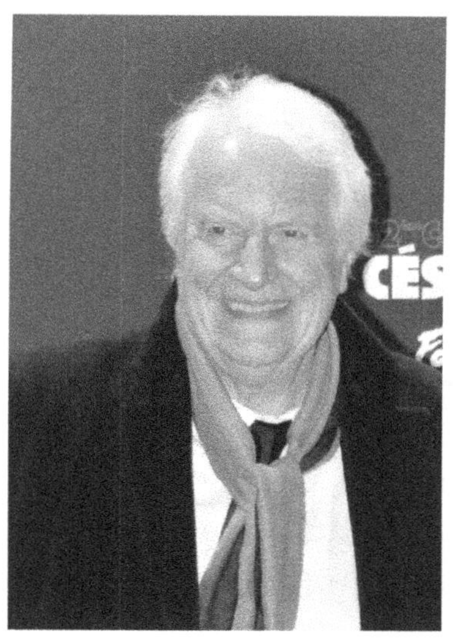

André Dussollier

At the time of the film's release, a number of critics drew comparisons between its plot and the classics of Alfred Hitchcock's cinema, including aspects of *Rear Window* (1954), *Vertigo* (1958), and *North by Northwest* (1959). Yet while the classic Hitchcockian scenario of investigating uncertain crimes which may – or may not – be taking place was certainly nothing new in and of itself, the creative decision to put dementia at the forefront of the action raises a whole host of interesting questions which help to make this unjustly neglected film stand out from the pack. How can Boyer solve such an ambiguous mystery when he cannot be certain of the accuracy of his own notebook's contents? Even if he can determine the culprit, will anyone believe his findings when they become aware of the condition which is affecting him? And, in the end, can he be sure that even the nature of his own identity is necessarily quite as fixed a concept as he once thought it to be? The agonised ex-policeman finds himself tortured over the unspoken issue that his loss of memory may actually be aiding the killer's plans... and eventually the audience may even find themselves asking if Boyer is, in fact, the killer himself.

While cinematic depictions of the dark underbelly of the City of Light are plentiful, including such memorable evocations as *Frantic* (Roman Polanski, 1988) and *Taken* (Pierre Morel, 2008), Boukhrief takes care to add a sense of disorientation and foreboding to proceedings, ensuring that the audience shares something of Boyer's unease, trepidation, and sensory confusion. Boukhrief's knowledge of classic cinema is no surprise given his career, which has included extensive journalism on cinematic theory and criticism as well as his creation of *The Newspaper of the Cinema* on the Canal+ channel in 1990. At that point arguably best-known for his film *Le Convoyeur* (2004), Boukhrief laces his film with plentiful allusions to earlier French cinema such as *Les Espions* (Henri-Georges Clouzot, 1957) and *Carte Vermeille* (Alain Levent, 1981). Although he exercises great economy in his direction, injecting just the right level of uncertainty regarding the supporting characters and their often-obscure motivations, it is Dussollier's outstanding evocation of insecurity, anger, and fear which leaves the greatest lasting impression.

In articulating Boyer's melange of competing feelings and his struggle against delirium, Dussollier crafts a character who is both believable and relatable. From his investigations, we are left in no doubt of Boyer's far-reaching intellect and skillset, which makes all the more poignant the fact that he is achingly aware of his gradual loss of mental capacity. While his dementia diagnosis is, of course, crucial to the mounting uncertainty surrounding the film's central plot, this atypical hero is never employed in an emotionally manipulative way; *Cortex* is a deeply human film, and the issue of individual dignity and autonomy is very much at its core. While some reviewers bemoaned the fact that the film's abrupt conclusion robs the audience of a truly satisfying sense of closure, others were quick to note that the suddenness of the *denouement* added impact to the fractured, piecemeal nature of Boyer's investigations, underscoring that life – in much the same manner as art – very rarely transpires in exactly the way that is anticipated.

Another reason for *Cortex*'s effectiveness is its excellent supporting cast. Julien Boisselier is highly effective as Thomas, Boyer's concerned son. Having earlier experience as a performer in Boukhrief's earlier cinema, Boisselier's thoughtful take on the character of the younger Boyer adds considerable depth to Dussolier's portrayal; Charles's concern for his son is entirely believable, as is his worry that his rapidly diminishing capacity will prove to be too much for Thomas to handle. Yet perhaps most successful of all are the other denizens of The Residénce, played by Aurore Clément and Gilles Gaston Dreyfus in the roles of Marie and Louis, and of course Marthe Keller as the crucial figure of Carole Rothmann. All of these characters, in their own way, emphasise that everyone has their own way of coping with life at the residential home, and their individual approaches aid in delineating the disordered nature of Boyer's attempts to come to terms with his new living conditions as well as his changing mental state. Dussolier and Keller had famously appeared together in Claude Lelouch's celebrated *Toute Une Vie* (1974), and here – more than thirty years later – they evoke an entirely different aspect of their earlier chemistry. Pascal Elbé also impresses as the enigmatic Docteur Chenot, bringing an understated tinge of glacial scientific distance to the part.

The murky oppressiveness of the film's clinical environment is well realised, as is its sterility and impersonal nature, and the script demonstrates astute (if often subtle) criticism towards the insensitive way that society can too often treat its elderly, infirm, and mentally impaired. However, for all the worthiness of its social commentary it is the originality of *Cortex*'s central concept that ensures continued audience interest. In an age where youth predominates in popular cinema, a film which features a totally compelling central performance from an outstanding actor in the later years of life should be commended as a breath of fresh air, not least when he is playing a character who is no lantern-jawed hero but rather a vulnerable but determined individual concerned only with doing the right thing while he still can – even when the impact of dementia means that this aim is far more nebulous and intangible than he had ever dared fear during his long career in law enforcement. In his prime, Boyer at least knew the enemy he was facing; as a result of his mental decline, even that certainty has been taken from him, meaning that – like the audience – he is forced to question everything he thought he knew about reasoning and analysis. Whether the endpoint of his investigations proves to be either surprising or predictable will largely depend on the viewer's familiarity with crime cinema, but there is no denying that *Cortex* is an arresting viewing experience, filled with ominous imagery, cunningly-employed red herrings, and a laudable sense of humanity.

6

FESTIVE THEMES AND CHRISTMAS MEMORIES

Chazz Palminteri's Noel

THERE are few genres of popular cinema quite so keenly geared towards an exploration of nostalgia than that of the Christmas movie. No other category of film encourages us to look back with fondness so readily, nor quite so unabashedly commends the virtues of kith and kin. Although various medical conditions have featured in Christmas films over the years (including mental health, in movies such as in George Seaton's 1947 classic *Miracle on 34th Street*), to date the issue of dementia remains almost completely unexplored within the genre. But when British Prime Minister David Cameron launched the *Christmas to Remember* digital campaign in December 2012, encouraging the public to share their own individual Christmas memories in order to highlight the issue of dementia over the festive season, he would have needed to look no further than Chazz Palminteri's underrated 2004 ensemble drama *Noel* if he sought a depiction of dementia care over the Christmas period and its implications for families and carers.

Noel is, by any critical standard, an unconventional film. Although ensemble features were slowly making a comeback in Christmas cinema by the mid-2000s, with successful features including romantic comedy *Love Actually* (Richard Curtis, 2003) and Christian Carion's wartime masterpiece *Joyeux Noël* (2005), rarely were they to be quite so eclectic in their choice of characters and scenarios than in this, Palminteri's big-screen directorial debut. Lurching from fantasy to domestic drama, and from light whimsy to high emotion, *Noel* employs a large and seemingly unconnected group of offbeat characters to explore a less-than-typical Christmas Eve in a snowy New York City (though the film was, in fact, actually filmed in Montreal). Nominally headlining the starry cast is Susan Sarandon as Rose Harrison, an editor at an inner-city publishing house whose personal life is dominated by the care of her elderly mother Helen (Una Kay), now in the late stages of Alzheimer's Disease. Much of the film's narrative concerns Rose's inability to forge friendships through a fear of jeopardising

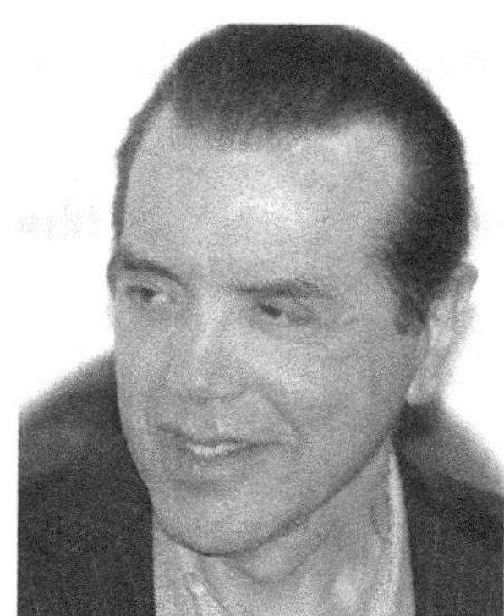
Chazz Palminteri

her availability to ensure her mother's ongoing personal care, even though Helen is receiving long-term treatment at a specialist ward of a city hospital.

Rose finds her life in a kind of involuntary stasis; acutely aware of her loneliness at Christmas, she struggles to cope with her mother's disorder and is reluctant to seek escape through romantic commitment. Yet Helen, though almost entirely unable to communicate by conventional means, eventually manages to convince her daughter that caring for a loved one does not preclude the forging of new personal relationships, and that the obligations of the present should not obscure the possibilities of the future. This eventually leads, albeit by unforeseen means, to a fledgling attraction between Rose and her mother's medical supervisor, the kindly Dr Baron (John Doman). Also guiding Rose through this emotional epiphany is Charlie Boyd (an uncredited and surprisingly low-key Robin Williams), a mysterious stranger at the hospital who is eventually revealed to have a hidden purpose that impacts significantly on Rose's life.

It is much to Palminteri's skill as a director, and also to the talents of screenwriter David Hubbard, that the many intersecting storylines of *Noel* never conspire to overpower the comparatively low-key tale of Rose's struggle to provide effective care during the holiday season. This seems particularly admirable given that her portion of the film's plot is competing with numerous others which feature some attention-grabbing characters, including the tempestuous romance between paralegal Nina (Penélope Cruz) and city cop Mike (Paul Walker), the plans of eccentric Jules (Marcus Thomas) to attend a hospital inpatients' Christmas party with his friend Glenn (Merwin Mondesir), and the curious case of deli waiter Artie (Alan Arkin) who turns out to be hiding a surprising secret.

Palminteri's ease behind the camera seems all the more remarkable given the fact that, until this point, his directorial experience had encompassed only a 1999 episode of HBO's television prison drama *Oz* (1997-2003) and a made-for-TV comedy, *Women vs Men*, which was aired by MGM Television in 2002. He takes care to portray dementia in a realistic light, emphasising the practical difficulties of the condition whilst stopping short of mawkishness in his depiction of Rose's difficulties as a caregiver. There are many poignant touches in this sympathetic interpretation, not least some superbly judged set decoration by Frances Calder, Suzanne Cloutier and Marie-Claude Gosselin, who exhibit incredible attention to detail in bringing Helen's hospital room – potentially a bleak and antiseptic environment – to life in effective and often unexpected ways, including fine details such as a range of assorted framed family photographs bedecking the walls by way of a reminiscence aid.

Noel's multi-character approach, in which a broad range of seemingly disparate individuals find themselves entangled due to a variety of unanticipated incidents, owes more to the ensemble dramas of Robert Altman than the average festive movie. Yet the film is indisputably a Christmas feature at heart, and not only as a result of its Yuletide setting. While it would not be unreasonable to venture the opinion that *Noel* is among the least orthodox of Christmas films in recent years, even in a decade where traditional genre boundaries were being challenged and overlapped as never before, it nonetheless demonstrated an ability to advance particular narrative themes in a manner which was genuinely remarkable. It is a film which blends oddball comedy with moving pathos, and contrasts emotional drama with perceptive character observations. As had been the case with so many other yuletide features before it, *Noel* emphasises the potential for the festive season to foster rebirth, personal transformation, and the potential strength of the community. Linking each of the film's individual stories is an exploration of love, be it romantic (Nina and Mike, Rose and Dr Baron), familial (Artie and Paul, Rose and Helen), emotional (Charlie and Rose, Jules and his abandonment issues), or spiritual (Charlie and his affecting search for his lost faith). There are various motifs which connect these tales, most prominent among them angel ornaments – in this particular context, a symbol of faith in better times yet to come. Mike breaks the glass angel on Nina's tree, which is eventually replaced by Artie's, while Rose

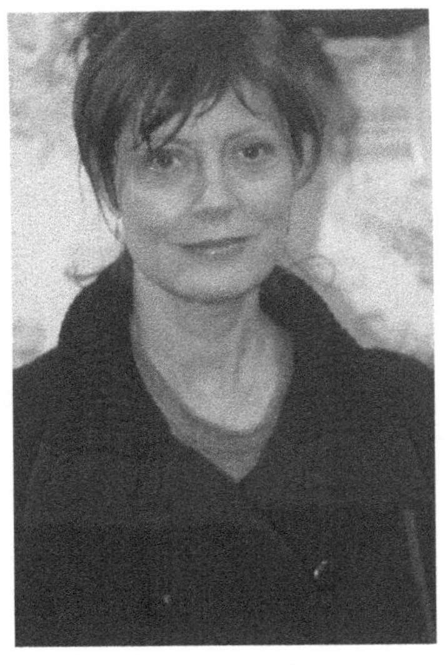

Susan Sarandon

buys a renaissance angel for Helen and ends up presenting it as a gift to Charlie instead. Even that stalwart of the festive season, the Christmas tree, can be seen to crop up regularly throughout the narrative; when Mike's temper causes him to wreck the tree that Nina has set up for him, he unwittingly mirrors the incident that had derailed Artie's life in the seventies, while Nina makes her pregnancy revelation next to a decorated fir tree and Rose's rather maudlin open-mike performance causes her to win a rather sorry-looking plastic tree, which she later gifts to her mother as an early Christmas present.

Connecting all of the film's stories is a search for affirmation. In Rose's case, her devotion to her mother has caused her to isolate herself from almost everyone around her, while the subsequent failure of her marriage and the sadness that she feels about her lack of motherhood has led her to question the direction of her life – an existential crisis that has reached a fever pitch as she nears middle age. Only the sudden intervention of Charlie (who himself is attempting to reconnect with a sense of religious faith that once meant so much to him) can convince her to reach out and unite with the world again, stalling her efforts to desperately shut out other people. Sarandon's touching, thoughtful performance is balanced perfectly by Una Kay's meticulously underplayed appearance as her onscreen mother Helen, while Williams was on excellent form in a quietly contemplative role, cast against type to remarkable effect.

With its emphasis on the search for a sense of belonging, the importance of family and the need for individual redemption, *Noel* is a film which typifies many primary concerns of the Christmas film genre. And yet, with its overlapping stories and evocation of an urban mood during a thoroughly contemporary holiday season, it also employs the conventions of the ensemble drama to good effect, making the most of its diverse and impressive cast. Although *Noel*'s nonconformist approach has made it something of a curio amongst Christmas films since its release, it can be seen as part of a wider movement at the time towards a more particular engagement with themes of love and redemption, utilising an ensemble framework, within a festively-situated narrative – one which would lead to other successful, if rather more conventional, multi-character romantic dramas later in the decade, such as *The Holiday* (Nancy Meyer, 2005) and *Four Christmases* (Seth Gordon, 2008).

Noel is undeniably an acquired taste, and in the grand tradition of many other Altman-esque ensemble dramas of a similar type it contains the occasional character who appears to have wandered into the film more or less by mistake. Nonetheless, at its best *Noel* does a worthy job of typifying the contradictory feelings inherent in a caring role: loneliness and isolation rub shoulders with compassion and optimism, thanks in no small part to David Hubbard's estimably nuanced screenplay. The film may stray quite some distance from more conventional festive fare, but for an empathetic and well-disposed depiction of dementia care at Christmas it remains worthy of note.

7 SATIRICAL APPROACHES AND DEMENTIA CLICHES

South Park's Grey Dawn

ANIMATED television has brought the world no end of social satire over recent decades, with increasingly sophisticated cultural lampoonery emanating from series as varied as Matt Groening's *The Simpsons* (1989-), Mike Judge and Greg Daniels's *King of the Hill* (1997-2010), and Seth MacFarlane's *Family Guy* (1999-). However, rarely has the edge of animated satire proven to be quite as razor-sharp as in the regular helpings of irreverent commentary served up by Comedy Central's long-running series *South Park*.

Since its network premiere in August 1997, *South Park* has gleefully cannoned headlong into subjects of immense controversy which, over the years, have included assisted suicide, the War on Terror, abortion, and race relations. So with such an extensive and fearless pedigree of notoriety, it seemed only inevitable that dementia would eventually come into the sights of the series' creators... and, when the moment arrived, they dealt with the issue through a characteristic blend of contentious wit and thoughtful observation.

The frenetic action of *South Park* takes place from the point of view of four adolescent friends who live in the eponymous fictional mountain town in Colorado. Created by Trey Parker and Matt Stone, the series has been no stranger to contention, its choice of subject matter being lauded and derided in equal measure by critics and cultural commentators even up to the present day. *South Park* has, however, developed a proven track record of encouraging meaningful debate about many weighty social issues, leading to several awards and nominations over the years including the prestigious Primetime Emmys. Some have praised the series' slyly incisive reflections on modern life, while others attack its relentless undermining of authority and cultural shibboleths. But if there is one thing that a majority will agree on, it is that *South Park* has often proven to be very difficult to ignore.

Arguably the series' most notable brush with the subject of dementia took place in 'Grey Dawn', the tenth episode of the series' seventh season, which was broadcast in November 2003. Deliberately diving in at the deep end, 'Grey Dawn' begins by tackling the sensitive question of how road safety can best be ensured in the driving skills of elderly people. When a number of pedestrian casualties are caused by mature drivers around the town of South Park, the state requires everyone over the age of seventy to relinquish their licences to the Department of Motor Vehicles. It is heavily hinted, though not addressed explicitly, that the drivers in question are affected by a decline in cognitive function which has affected their physical reactions as well as their skills of observation. Outraged by this perceived violation of his human rights, one of the elderly citizens of South Park promptly calls in the American Association of Retired Persons (AARP) to negotiate on his behalf.

As the episode's title suggests, the plot then advances into an all-out parody of John Milius's notorious Cold War paranoia thriller *Red Dawn* (1984). In that taut suspense film, a group of American teenagers were forced to defend their town in a guerrilla conflict against a combined invasion of Communist forces from the Soviet Union, Nicaragua, and Cuba. Fast-forwarding two decades, the *South Park* version of this dark fable sees the AARP invading the town and corralling everyone of middle-age and younger into makeshift prison camps, in direct retaliation for the ban on elderly drivers. With typically surreal *South Park* amplification, a political pressure group set up to represent the rights of senior citizens is ultimately depicted as a paramilitary organisation with revolutionary intent. The four main characters are forced into nearby woodlands where they must formulate a plan to overcome heavily-armed AARP members and restore order, thus setting in motion a conclusion which is replete with the kind of cheerfully warped logic that *South Park* has always excelled at employing.

For a series which has relentlessly ridiculed organisations on every point of the political spectrum – to say nothing of satirising organised religion, spirituality, and atheism with equal zeal – it is intriguing to see just how guardedly reticent *South Park* proves to be when dealing with the subject of dementia. Although the condition is hardly ever mentioned by name, it is obvious from its repeated depiction of diminished capacity and memory loss that dementia – not the possible risks to road safety that are potentially caused by elderly drivers (including conceivable threats to themselves) – is in fact the real focus of the episode. However, even given the frankness of approach that is characteristically applied by the *South Park* writing team, the subject of mental health is dealt with almost coyly in 'Grey Dawn'. The episode's depiction of dementia is amalgamated – and thus diluted – with deliberately generalised banalities surrounding senior citizens' concerns which are deployed for comic effect (such as repeated complaints about teenagers skateboarding in public areas).

In a manner common to the series, 'Grey Dawn' takes a central issue of significance and then situates it in a consciously over-the-top narrative – in this case, one which borrows effectively from

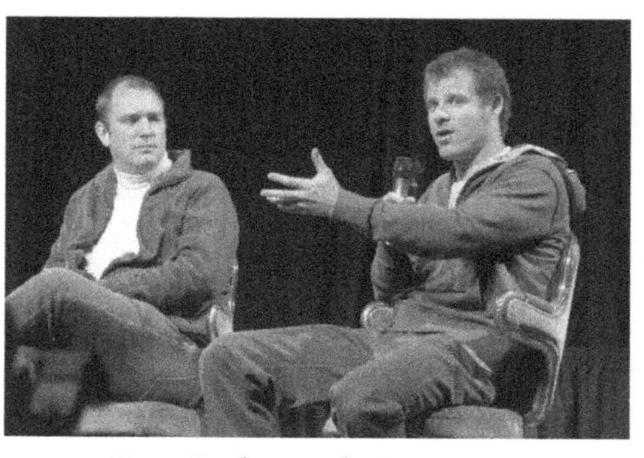

Trey Parker and Matt Stone

the stylistic tropes of the horror and survivalist thriller genres to make its point through premeditated absurdity. Elderly people armed with machine guns work to empty care homes of residents as though liberating them from captivity, strongly challenging negative preconceptions about the attitudes and capabilities of senior citizens which are all too often unthinkingly disseminated by some corners of the mass media. Yet while this may seem a refreshing and emboldening depiction of people in their later years, paradoxically the episode itself is often just as guilty of reproducing many of the same fixed notions that it is attacking; for instance, when one elderly man is told that the revolution has arrived his immediate response is that he had 'better get his other sweater' before taking up arms.

While watching a succession of rocket launcher-toting senior citizens moving beyond the confines of their home town with the ultimate intention of taking over the United States by force is certainly amongst the least conventional television narratives to feature dementia, *South Park*'s take on unconstructive and patronising views of the elderly is no less effective for its eccentricity. There are genuine flashes of resentment on the part of the series' writers with regard to the unfair treatment of older people; condescending dialogue directed towards the town's elderly residents and indirect allusions to voluntary euthanasia and limitations imposed upon personal autonomy all combine to produce a barbed satire which ultimately leaves audiences unsure about who they should be sympathising with.

South Park has dealt with elderly characters and issues deriving from the ageing process even from its formative years, with several early episodes centring around Stan Marsh's cantankerous (and often somewhat nihilistic) grandfather. Yet its relative temerity surrounding issues deriving from dementia has largely continued, even as recently as Ubisoft's successful spin-off videogame *South Park: The Fractured but Whole* (2017), which features prominent mission-critical scenes – and even a prolonged combat sequence – at the town's 'Shady Acres' residential home. Here, players find themselves encountering many of the usual truisms deriving from the series' elderly characters – confusion over taking the correct medication, misunderstandings caused by memory loss, and so on – counterbalanced with considerably more inspired humour, such as when the schoolkids who make up the regular cast arrive to perform a musical number for the residents only to be met with derision and impatience from their audience rather than the stereotypical delight of older people being entertained by the talents of young children that mainstream expectation suggests that we should anticipate. Here too, however, the player is faced with something of a missed opportunity; the symptoms of dementia are framed more as a risk of growing older than as an existential hazard that is, in fact, capable of reshaping any life, thus reinforcing a long-held misapprehension rather than defying anticipated audience responses – a strategy which the series has employed to great effect, and even excelled at, when at its best.

Over the years, *South Park* has succeeded in examining difficult subjects in an uncompromising way, and the conclusions that are drawn throughout 'Grey Dawn' may prove awkward viewing for anyone who still holds to strong considerations about the way that senior citizens and people who are affected by dementia should be depicted on television. The series may not be easily confused with high art, but for a twenty-minute slice of animated comedy it is commendable that its creators have made an attempt to encourage careful thought about how people are treated in later life by popular culture, in addition to promoting interpersonal respect between individuals of all ages. Certainly there is little doubt about the unambiguous subtext that people should neither be taken for granted nor subject to lazy generalisations, irrespective of how long they have lived. However, by making a point of confronting stereotypes while simultaneously falling back upon the occasional tired maxim even as the script hammers home its point, 'Grey Dawn' can be considered only a qualified success.

8

ELIMINATING THE IMPOSSIBLE

Mitchell and Webb, Sherlock Holmes and Dementia

THERE are few things in life quite so subjective as comedy, and few comic double-acts of recent years have proven to be quite as divisive as that of David Mitchell and Robert Webb. Active on TV and radio since the mid-nineties, and perhaps still best-known for their controversial, squirm-inducing Channel 4 sitcom *Peep Show* (2003-15), the pair are no strangers to edgy humour, and were at the forefront of the 'comedy of embarrassment' which dominated the noughties – a wave of socially-awkward humour spurred on by the efforts of other high-profile performers such as Ricky Gervais in the BBC's *The Office* (2001-03) and the improvisations of Sacha Baron Cohen in the guise of his characters Ali G, Borat Sagdiyev, and Brüno Gehard on Channel 4's

The 11 O'Clock Show (1998-2000) and *Da Ali G Show* (2000-04). However, in spite of their ready engagement with contentious subject matter throughout their careers, it took until the production of their BBC sketch-show *That Mitchell and Webb Look* (2006-10) before they would address the issue of dementia... and, when they did so, it was to be in the least conventional of ways.

That Mitchell and Webb Look split opinion even amongst the duo's most die-hard fans, with many finding the self-conscious deviation from the anxious, discomfiting contemporary realism of *Peep Show* to be stylistically jarring. Featuring a varied range of sketches, many of which called upon a nostalgic, backward-looking view of popular culture (including parodies of *Terry and June*-style situation comedy and *Carry On* film-inspired bawdy humour) as well as that of modern TV staples such as surreal quiz shows and off-the-wall reality programmes, the series proved to be an acquired taste for many. Despite critical discord amongst the nation's cultural commentators, however, *That Mitchell and Webb Look* went on to win a BAFTA television award, and has been broadcast worldwide as well as subsequently released on home entertainment formats. With a healthy audience and a dedicated fan following, their take on dementia was therefore guaranteed to garner attention, and in the tradition of their most prominent material the sketch was to subvert expectation by leaving the public unsure exactly how to react to its premise.

Featuring in an episode which concluded the fourth series of the programme, first broadcast in 2010, Mitchell and Webb present us with Sherlock Holmes (played by Mitchell) in a state of advanced age. Now resident in a nursing home designed to mimic his famous rooms at 221B Baker Street, he is visited every day by his devoted friend Dr John Watson (Webb) who tries his utmost to convince his ailing colleague that he is still in his prime. In the style of much of the writers' retro-seventies material, the sketch is free from the trappings of political correctness and – at least initially – is guaranteed to offend anyone who works with, or has ever had direct involvement with, someone who has dementia. There are deeply unsubtle jokes about incontinence, memory loss, and difficulty with identifying close acquaintances. Modern design principles relating to dementia are co-opted into the sketch; the door of Holmes's room consists of the digits 221 followed by a picture of a bee, to signify his illustrious address in a manner that is more readily recognisable to him in his current state of cognitive decline. To further reinforce the negative effects of dementia upon Holmes, Scotland Yard's Inspector Lestrade arrives to request the great

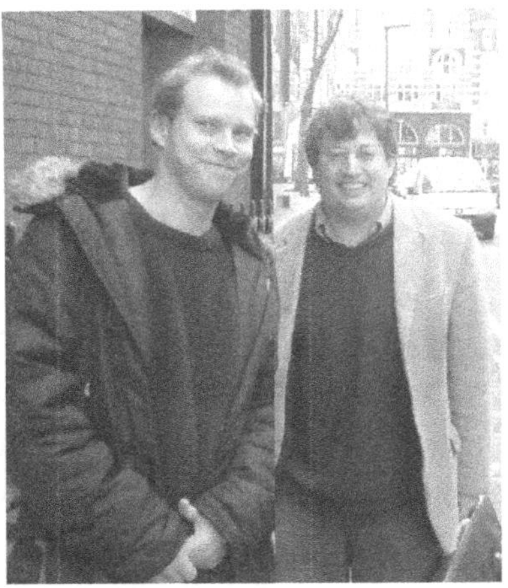

Robert Webb and David Mitchell

detective's assistance on a complicated case, only to discover that the older man is experiencing major difficulties with basic tasks such as eating and drinking. The Inspector and Watson watch in quiet despondency, realising that the once-brilliant Holmes's days of world-class detection are now at an end.

But just when the entire sketch seems doomed towards simply restating outmoded and insulting truisms about dementia, something unexpected happens. In a moment of poignant sadness which occurs just before the episode's climax, Holmes has a heart-rending instance of lucidity. After several minutes of underscoring just how much this soaring intellect has been deleteriously affected by dementia, the canned laughter suddenly falls silent. Drained and resigned, Holmes confides to Watson that he is entirely aware of the nature of his condition and knows all too well that his mental capacity is deteriorating rapidly. It is as though a mist has descended upon him, he mutters quietly, lamenting that he is completely unable to see through it. The look which passes between the two men speaks of both distress and inevitability. His old companion Watson is at a loss, unsure how to respond, as the scene fades to black.

This total shift in emphasis may make for uncomfortable and unanticipated viewing, but it is highly effective in its execution. The first three-quarters of the sketch sees Holmes repeatedly humiliated, his legendary skills of deduction blunted by a condition which is entirely beyond his control. Mitchell and Webb's choice of Arthur Conan Doyle's celebrated character seems entirely deliberate; Sherlock Holmes remains one of the most cerebral of literary figures, and more than many others he stands to be profoundly affected by any decline in his cognitive powers. Yet for those willing to look beyond the acute tastelessness of the sketch's opening gambit, there appears to be a deeper message at work.

Having employed just about every imaginable dementia-related cliché throughout the sketch for comic effect, suddenly the viewer is reminded that this is a real condition which is affecting an ailing human being... and that he is powerless to do anything about it. If dementia can impact so intensely upon the mental wellbeing of even an intellectual grandmaster like Holmes, the audience are informed, then it has just as much chance of affecting the viewers themselves, or someone close to them. In the blink of an eye, Watson is precipitously transformed from a comic stooge into a concerned and thoughtful companion, the relationship between Holmes and himself being developed into something much more significant during those closing moments. His role has shifted from professional associate to concerned friend, even a compassionate carer. Public familiarity with this timeless crime-fighting duo further bolsters the moving nature of the situation as it is presented.

The premise of Sherlock Holmes battling dementia would later become key to Bill Condon's innovative mystery film *Mr Holmes* (2015), a cinematic adaptation of Mitch Cullin's novel *A Slight Trick of the Mind* (2005) which featured Ian McKellen as Conan Doyle's great detective, now living in retirement in Sussex at the age of 93. Struggling against cognitive decline and relying on herbal remedies (such as the jelly from a prickly ash plant recovered from post-war Hiroshima) in an attempt to counter his memory loss, Holmes has difficulty coping in the world of 1947 and becomes increasingly reliant on his housekeeper and her inquisitive, intellectually-gifted son. Much of the film is concerned with Holmes's discontent with Dr Watson's fictionalisation of their last case together, though his fragmented memories make it virtually impossible for him to determine the root of his discomfiture with Watson's literary account. Eventually, through the unconscious prompting that his companions provide, Holmes is eventually able to piece together the disparate incidents which made up 'The Adventure of the Dove Grey Glove', though ultimately he finds only despondency as he discovers the truth which lies behind the case, and as the narrative continues he has no choice but to face up to the reality of his growing mental and physical decline.

While Condon's film, and Cullin's novel which inspired it, will likely be the take on Holmes and dementia that will endure longest in the public eye, Mitchell and Webb's sketch nonetheless makes a similar point about the effects of the condition on even the most brilliant mind with greater economy – and no less devastating impact. Many people may find it difficult to watch, and for some the bad taste of the initial premise will not justify the sentiment which lies behind its conclusion. However, by building up a deliberately hackneyed portrayal of dementia only to demolish it so powerfully, Mitchell and Webb seem determined to attack the very kind of languid assumptions that they parody so relentlessly in their opening gambit. The audience, having been prepared to expect a particular pay-off, find themselves with an unforeseen conclusion which is genuinely disconcerting when first encountered, but it is one which challenges viewers to think carefully about what they have been laughing at, and to deliberate conscientiously upon whether they should reconsider their initial response.

Music

9

STOKING THE FLAMES OF REMEMBRANCE

Ed Sheeran's Afire Love

ED Sheeran has proven to be one of Britain's most successful recording artists of recent years; a star with a meteoric rise whose chart-topping achievements and modest, unassuming manner have won him countless fans across the country and far beyond. Originally hailing from Framlingham in Suffolk, the ubiquitous musician has scooped several major industry awards over the past few years, his plaudits including wins at the Brit, Ivor Novello and Q Awards, alongside armful of nominations for prizes as prestigious as the MOBO, Grammy and MTV Video Music Awards. In 2017, he was appointed a Member of the Order of the British Empire (MBE) in the UK Birthday Honours List, for services to both music and charity. His studio album + (2011) has received platinum status on six occasions by the British Phonographic Industry, topping music charts all around the globe, while his 2014 album release *X* topped the UK album charts and the Billboard chart in the US, selling more than eight and a half million copies worldwide to date. His most recent studio album, ÷ (2017), was to become Spotify's most-streamed album of the year, having been played more than 3.1 billion times. It became the best-selling album in both the UK and US throughout 2017, winning him the Global Success Award at the 2018 Brit Awards and cementing him as one of the world's best-selling musicians. At time of writing, he has sold in excess of 26 million albums, and over 100 million singles.

Much critical interest has surrounded 'Afire Love', the twelfth track to appear on *X*, Sheeran's second studio album which was released in June 2014. The song was composed by Sheeran in memory of his late grandfather, who had been affected by Alzheimer's Disease for a period of twenty years. As recounted in many interviews at the time of the album's release, Sheeran was very close to his grandfather while growing up and began writing the song only two weeks before the older man's death, completing it at the time of his funeral. Thus the song could not fail to be an emotional account of a life lived well, of a man beloved by his family who had fought a long battle against illness.

Sheeran has never been an artist to shy away from controversial subject matter. His songs, often performed at very high-profile events, have dealt with issues as hard-hitting and divisive as alcohol abuse and abortion.

Thus he addresses the issue of Alzheimer's Disease with characteristic candour, never shrinking from the emotional turbulence that can – and does – affect the friends and family of a person who has dementia, as well as the person affected by the condition themselves.

'Afire Love' initially considers dementia in terms which have become familiar in song-writing and poetry – a thief of memory, cast in the guise of some sort of vaguely demonic presence which can be fought valiantly but yet is never truly defeated. However, before he can brush too close to the territory of the hackneyed maxim, Sheeran shifts emphasis and turns the song's sentiment on its head. The listener quickly becomes aware that this is not a work about a man who was overpowered and subjugated by illness, but rather someone who lived a full life in spite of it. Sheeran's grandfather, we are left in no doubt, was a family man who meant the world to those around him, and this is the message that Sheeran spends the most time conveying. Dementia, we hear through his lyrics, may have diminished his grandfather's mental capacity, but it could not loosen the bonds of devotion which made him mean so much to the people who loved him right to the end of his life.

Sheeran effectively employs a juxtaposition of light and dark throughout the song, a motif with which he contrasts funereal black with the brightness of the sun, of life, of the inner being. Thus the dim opacity of dementia's veil is pierced by an innate power that transcends anything with which the disease can deploy to confront it. We hear of Sheeran's grandmother voicing

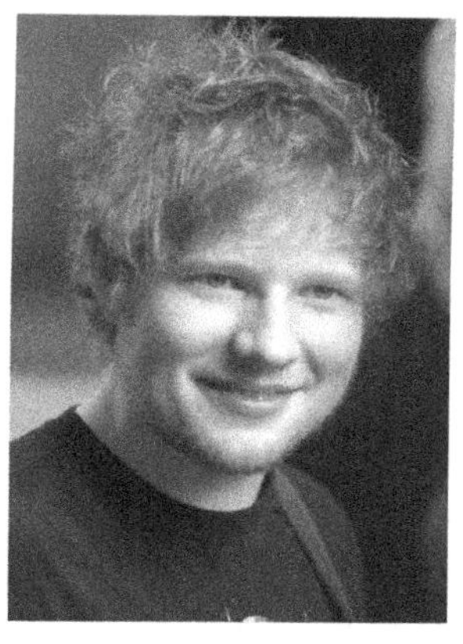
Ed Sheeran

her regrets over her husband's ailing memory, and then become acutely aware of a union of love which cannot be denied – not by dementia, nor even by death. Given the nature of such an affecting topic, to say nothing of the circumstances of its composition, a degree of emotional rawness would seem inevitable. Yet this is not a song which is mawkish or laboured in the articulation of its subject matter. Sheeran manages to balance with great skill and confidence the heartache of loss with the celebration of life, reminding us that he seeks to rejoice in a unique life rather than reduce his loved one to a mere discussion of medical symptoms.

'Afire Love' is a song which dexterously shifts from the nostalgic to the contemporary; in a way, mirroring the tendency of dementia to rob individuals of a sense of the present, flitting instead between the concerns of the immediate and the events of long ago. Through Sheeran's recollections, and those of his family members, we witness his grandfather's experiences being brought to life in a manner that is reflected through the affection and high regard in which he was so obviously held. We see the efforts of the medical profession to preserve life meeting with limited success even in spite of their best intentions, while the declining health of Sheeran's grandfather is filtered through reminiscences of golden sunshine and summer warmth in a way which combats the clinical environment of his final days. Even in the funereal scenes which conclude the song, Sheeran is quick to emphasise the ability of love, family and community to hold the ravages of disease at bay. The cold rain which accompanies his grandfather's burial stands in stark contrast to the idealised summertime which tinged recollections of the early romance which we hear being formed between him and his wife. Similarly, the dreary weather at the event can do nothing to blunt the sense of triumphant celebration, hailing the life of a good man whose final days would not be allowed to delineate him or his legacy amongst those who loved him.

While it is true that medicine does not currently hold the key to reversing or preventing the onset of dementia, here we are shown that it can be dominated by other, less conventional means – by refusing to allow the damaging effects of its symptoms to erode our own memories of the person who is affected by them. Thus we see, again and again, the observance of a good man who gave love and was loved, who valued his friends and family and who was cherished by them in return. Sheeran's song is also inclusive enough to inspire people irrespective of whether they adhere to spiritual beliefs or reject them in favour of material rationalism; whether one has faith in a post-corporeal existence (as Sheeran's lyrics hint near the beginning of the song) or instead believes that death is the definitive end of an individual's conscious being, there is no denying the overarching sense of release that 'Afire Love' brings to the realisation that the relative in question has now been freed from the damage wrought by the disease afflicting him, and that its effects can finally bear upon him no longer. What happens after life, the song appears to suggest, is less important than how we conducted ourselves amongst those around us. It is a strikingly affirmative sentiment, to consider that life should be lived to its fullest potential irrespective of personal circumstances, and naturally it is a directive that will mean different things to different people – in addition to being considered the kind of constructive, encouraging attitude that is intended to unify rather than divide.

'Afire Love' is a song which challenges audiences to examine their own attitudes towards dementia, as well as each other. While we come to know Sheeran's grandfather through the lens of failing health, equally we are shown that this is only one part of the story, not all of it. This is a song which calls attention to the triumph of hope over despair, and of love over adversity. In equal parts touching and thought-provoking, 'Afire Love' is a work which seems to have been composed precisely to subvert expectations, and Sheeran takes care to counter assumptions because he is at pains to emphasise the uniqueness of the individual self over the way that people affected by dementia are so often reduced to the status of a faceless statistic by official reports and accounts of mainstream media reporting. It is obvious that he wants his audience to know that, in his view, dementia is something which impacts upon identity but should not ever be allowed to inform identity. It may be a condition which deeply changed his grandfather's life, but it has not changed his family's love and support for this beloved person. And this, perhaps, is the song's most memorable aspect: the emphasis that every life is unique, that every person connects with – and impacts upon – those around them, and that in all events hope persists and should be nurtured wherever possible.

10

IN SEARCH OF LOST MEMORIES

Jill Sobule's Claire

DEMENTIA remains, at present, a relatively uncommon subject for popular song-writing. However, the condition's increasing incidence across the world has led to it penetrating the public consciousness in ways which have gradually led to progressively more insightful and provocative treatment of the subject in all forms of popular media. The world of music is no exception, as can be witnessed in American singer-songwriter Jill Sobule's sensitive and provocative song 'Claire'.

Sobule has been active in the music industry since the mid-eighties, though her profile was significantly enhanced as a result of her contributions to the soundtrack of Amy Heckerling's *Clueless* (1995), a hugely successful teen romantic comedy which starred Alicia Silverstone. Over the years, Sobule's song-writing has skilfully blended some of the most evocative elements of folk and rock to produce memorable listening experiences which can often be uplifting but, in most cases, range from the contemplative to the hard-hitting. 'Claire' is one such song. Co-written by Sobule and Robin Eaton, the track first appeared on the 2004 album *Pink Pearl*, and has since earned no small amount of admiration on account of its thoughtful, respectful approach to its subject matter.

While she has become well-known for her sensitive, often impassioned ballads, Sobule is arguably better recognised for her insightful character studies which pair an astute narrative structure with moments of perceptive and often poignant awareness. These songs are often of an autobiographical nature (or, at the very least, contain diffuse autobiographical elements), but in many cases she places her focus firmly upon individual figures and their needs, feelings, and struggles. Though her work is often bitingly satirical, and informed by strong opinions about politics and the need for greater fairness and equality, she sometimes eschews such ideological and thematic concerns in favour of a more direct approach to the character study, delineating individual traits and unique aspects of personality to build a compelling picture of what it means to be human in a world that sometimes seems to exist in a near-permanent state of socio-cultural flux.

'Claire' is a song which concerns an elderly woman – the eponymous protagonist of the title – who has lived a full and varied life, but now finds that she has difficulty recalling the exact details of the many encounters and incidents that she has experienced over the years. The narrator's role is unclear; she may be a friend or a care professional, but it is clear that she visits Claire on a regular basis – though Claire is not always able to recognise the visitor, meaning that the narrator's presence is not always welcomed. On the occasions when it is, however, she is regaled with vibrant tales of Claire's life during the 1940s – her various loves, her part in the war effort, and even recollections of her skills as an aviator. There is little doubt of the older woman's independence and her trail-blazing attitude of free-thinking autonomy within the stifling conformity and patriarchal hierarchy evident in the repressive world of her youth.

Though the narrator enjoys hearing these accounts, she is unsure of the extent to which she can believe their accuracy; some experiences may have been unintentionally conflated, while there is a chance that others have been invented in their entirety – either intentionally or inadvertently. The excitement of the events which shaped Claire's early life is contrasted throughout the song with the difficulties that she is encountering in the present day, where memory loss has led to problems with performing everyday activities – difficulties which sometimes lead to her involuntarily putting herself at risk. As the song ends, the narrator reflects on how much that she wishes she could have known the younger Claire

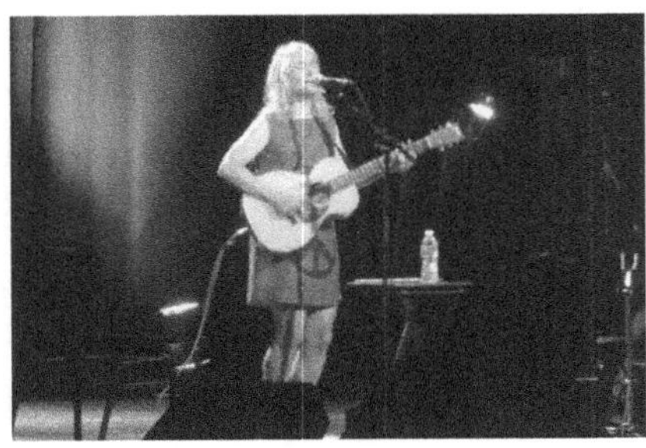

Jill Sobule

and joined in the wonderful experiences of her early life... only to reflect that Claire herself, in her later years, probably feels exactly the same way – now a stranger even to her own memories.

Although the song never directly makes mention of any specific form of dementia, its wistful suggestion of stolen reminiscence – of misremembered experience and bittersweet, possibly unreliable commentary – is powerfully contrasted with Claire's underlying frustration and sense of powerlessness. Sobule's contemplative performance of the song teases out contrasting strands of emotion with consummate skill, emphasising the effervescence of the character's formative years while never underplaying the melancholy of the present day; a time when even boiling a kettle can represent a task which carries an element of genuine risk.

Overall, however, 'Claire' is not an exercise in either despondency or sympathy, but rather a piece which is redolent with empathy, compassion, and a celebration of a remarkable life. Though the narrator seems unconvinced about the veracity of Claire's memories, it is clear that her misgivings are of little concern; what matters is the fact that Claire herself remembers the joy and exuberance of a remarkable youth and, even if her actual recollection may ultimately be at variance with the true facts (this possibility is hinted at but never explicitly resolved), she is still able to find comfort in the remembrance of a time and place far away from the here and now.

What seems particularly remarkable about Sobule's narrative voice throughout the song is the fact that, even when struggling to know which of Claire's accounts to believe and which to regard as misremembered recollections of long ago, the older woman is always treated with respect. When Claire candidly discusses her fluid sexuality, the narrator seems unsure whether to regard this as an aspect of her life which she had explored in her earlier days, or rather one which she had wanted to and yet had felt repressed by the restrictive social attitudes of the time from actually putting into practice. The important thing is that, in any respect, Claire is given the benefit of the doubt; surely what matters most is the fact that, if these experiences and characteristics are the ones by which she has chosen to define herself in the present day, that she is at liberty to do so.

There is a certain melancholy to Claire's observations that, during her discussions with the narrator, autumn appears to have arrived early that year. It is as though the earlier part of the year has become little more than a blur to her; interchangeable sequences of routine life which now appear so vague that, from her personal perspective, they may as well have happened to someone else. Yet it can also be seen to act as an allegory for her life in microcosm; a series of events and experiences which accumulated throughout her youth and middle-age that came to circumscribe the person that she was, only now subject to the erosion of time and dementia to the point that every aspect which made her unique has since become unreliable and essentially intangible.

It is with great insight that Sobule's narrator recognises that when Claire abruptly dismisses her, suddenly reaching a point where she no longer recognises the younger woman, that she is able to react with understanding rather than offence. Just as Claire's condition has rendered her memories unreliable, so too has it affected her social skills, meaning that even those who are close to her may unexpectedly appear unfamiliar, or even alarming. Yet this too forms a highly effective conclusion to the song, reinforcing the fact that life in Claire's world is very much shaped by the moment – something that she seems to share with her impulsive younger self, though now for very different reasons. What is important is that the narrator understands the need to recognise the fact that her elderly acquaintance is so profoundly affected by her condition that her unpredictable behaviour should not be subject to censure or disdain, but rather that the fundamental needs of the individual – who has no control over the speed or nature of her mental decline – must be acknowledged and acted upon.

Sobule is a songwriter who has proven herself entirely unafraid of dealing with contentious subject matter, and with 'Claire' she demonstrates a commendable willingness to engage with a complex condition in a manner which adeptly balances the euphoria of bygone youth with the discouragement caused by fractured memories and the infirmity of old age. Though engagement with these topics may not be widespread in popular music, Sobule proves that such themes may be presented in a way which neither sensationalises nor trivialises them. By her proficient juxtaposition, we see that there is no 'young' life or 'old' life – simply life itself, with all of its attendant joys and heartache. And in a world where the generation gap seems to grow wider with every passing year, her impassioned appeal for commonality and greater understanding between people of all ages is one which seems especially timely.

11

DETERMINING PERSONAS IN DYNAMIC SOUNDSCAPES

Brian Griffith's Memoirs of Dementia

OVER the years, musical compositions have been inspired by many motivating factors: romantic love, social injustice, cultural change, and heightened emotion have all proven to stimulate the creative impetus of musical talent in a variety of different ways. While dementia, and mental health in general, has proven to be a subject which is less readily engaged with by musicians, in recent years this trend is being actively challenged by recording artists who have demonstrated a willingness to confront misconceptions surrounding the condition as well as exploring the nature of its far-reaching effects upon those who are affected by it.

Brian James Griffith, who is also known by his performance name of Greyghost, is a Los Angeles-based experimental musician with a flair for unconventional approaches towards demanding topics. Co-founder of music collective Screaming Claws, Griffith has perhaps become best-known for his bass guitar recordings; he has used the instrument to great effect in creating ambient, immersive environments which rely both upon improvisational skill and acoustic ecology. In collaboration with fellow musician Angela Wilson, he has become recognised – particularly throughout California – for his Electric Sound Bath meditations, a characteristically inventive approach to sonic reflection and articulation which conveys manifold aspects of the emotional energy emanating from his audience. His thoughtful, meditative approach to performance has seen his work featured in publications as diverse as *Pitchfork* magazine and *The New York Times*.

In 2012, Griffith released *Memoirs of Dementia*, a four-track album which had been inspired by the life experiences of his great-grandmother Francis. Witnessing the effects of dementia upon this beloved matriarchal figure, who slowly found her sense of identity and environmental orientation challenged and gradually worn away by the progression of the condition, Griffith's observations of her struggle with the disease led him to question the nature of a human being's place within linear reality, ultimately guiding him into asking just how far we can trust our instincts and experience when they have been compromised by forces which lie beyond our control.

Performed live at Franklin Village in Los Angeles, and improvised using a variety of musical instruments, *Memoirs of Dementia* drew upon the thematic baseline of Griffith's memories of his late relative – and her advancing deterioration over a number of years – to suggest the confusion and distress caused by the condition as well as the fractured perceptions brought about by its onset. Knowing all too well that his audience is not composed of passive listeners, Griffith drew from the synergy of the crowd to accentuate the universality of the soundscape that he created on stage. Further buttressing the nostalgic aspect of what is an essentially reflective work, the music was recorded and sold on analogue cassette tape – a particularly daring development given the ubiquity of high-bitrate digital downloads which are most commonly favoured by recording artists seeking an international audience. (It must be noted, however, that Griffith has subsequently released his music upon a number of popular download platforms across the Internet for wider consumption by the public.)

While lengthy tracks such as 'Nectar of the Eastern Gods' and 'Beyond the Black Field' evoke wistfulness along with soothing, contemplative moments of deliberation, they also subtly guide the individual's personal perception of the sound environment, mediating their individual relation to the ambient musical milieu while simultaneously encouraging them to explore the limits of their expectations with regard to how disorder and uncertainty can disrupt acuity towards what we recognise as a normative state of being. Other pieces, such as 'Flowing Spirit Jar' or the opening 'Purple Dye #5', more overtly explore aspects of incident and recollection, family connections and meaningful interactions with loved ones in the past. This is achieved through a pensive meander through bygone experience, deftly alternating between melancholy and abstraction; while the warmth of youthful reminiscence is at times almost tangible, the interpolation of despondency and occasional mystification means that there is no mistaking it for a simplistic, rose-tinted view of yesteryear.

If the aforementioned approach may appear to suggest a somewhat nebulous creative strategy, in actuality nothing could be further from the truth. Griffith's artistic *modus operandi* is one of great flair and confidence, liberally peppered with insightful observations not just focusing upon a mind besieged by the confusing and the unfamiliar, but also – at its best – upon the essentially shifting, unpredictable nature of the human condition. His music very effectively depicts the conflict between the rational and irrational, the unfettered self whose soaring freedom is curtailed by a malign force that cannot be defended against or easily defined. This motif of liberty attempting to preserve itself against the encroachment of a restrictive and essentially destructive influence is a particularly powerful one, as it mirrors the age-old conflict between personal independence and imposed conformity; self-determination is continually undermined or obscured by an outside force which slowly inveigles itself into the mindset of the person affected, meaning that the very concept of autonomy itself becomes fleeting and unreliable.

Memoirs of Dementia also excels in its depiction of dementia as a condition with an almost surreal capacity to obfuscate even the most straightforward aspects of life. Thus we become aware of long-held memories suddenly becoming untrustworthy, of moods shifting abruptly, and of old certainties being destabilised without warning. It is much to Griffith's credit, then, that there is no overriding sense of despair which conveys the impression of implacable invasion of turmoil and disarray, or indeed a melancholic reflection of the slow obliteration of the self. Such fatalistic concerns would have no place in a work where the commemoration of the uniqueness of the individual is very much at the forefront, and where the potential of life is valued and commended even when it is clearly under siege.

It could be argued that Griffith's most remarkable achievement lies in his ability to circumscribe the effects of dementia within deliberately vague but still workable terms. The listener finds themselves faced with an evocation of dementia which is, at a single stroke, both oppressive and chaotic; a phenomenon capable of subjugating all the possibilities of freedom while imposing, rather than a new form of order, a torrent of uncertainties which can make even the most familiar elements of life seem strange and outlandish. Naturally this dichotomy is demonstrated most keenly in Griffith's representation of the subtle yet devastating battle which rages between the comparative orderliness of past memories and the ability of dementia to disrupt their veracity, causing the series of events which combine to shape a life to suddenly appear erratic or even fallacious. It is testament to the power of Griffith's music that this gradual, injurious process is articulated with such perceptive skill, unfolding in a slow but seemingly inevitable progression. This makes his overarching theme – of celebrating life experiences even in the face of influences which have the capacity to destabilise and obliterate them – all the more potent and emotionally affecting.

With *Memoirs of Dementia*, Griffith was to create an unyielding, bittersweet work of musical art which juxtaposes the innocence of boyhood with the unbearable grief of loss – of his elderly relative's fading sense of self, her diminished ability to perceive the world around her, and ultimately his sorrow at the end of her life. There is much understated power employed in his minimalist instrumentation… and yet, given the weightiness of the subject matter, it is his use of light touches which linger longest in the mind of the listener. For every moment of dark contemplation, there is a corresponding incidence of playfulness or buoyancy; while we are left in no doubt of his forlorn sadness at the death of his great-grandmother, he seems determined to rejoice in her memory just as much as he laments her passing. And this, perhaps, is the underlying subtext of the album as a whole: that dementia has the ability to impact not only upon the person who is directly affected by it, but on everyone who is close to that individual. Griffith makes plain the lasting and significant effect that his relative's dementia had upon his childhood and young adulthood, shaping his anxieties about the essential fragility of perception and the self.

12 UNDERSTANDING THAT TRANSCENDS GENERATIONS

Harry Gardner's Not Alone

IT seems somewhat ironic that, even after years of public awareness campaigns by dementia organisations and charities, the condition is often still wrongly depicted by many works as an inevitable risk of growing old, when in fact there are many incidences of its onset affecting people within different age groups. Similarly, dementia has an impact not just upon the person who has been diagnosed with it, but also on those close to them – family and friends who are of all ages, and who may each react to the condition in different ways. This intergenerational aspect of dementia has, until recently, too often been overlooked. However, the issue – and the manner in which it had been wrongly neglected – was to be vigorously addressed in 2016 with the release of 'Not Alone', a song by teenager Harry Gardner.

The release of 'Not Alone: Song for Alzheimer's' was to generate significant press coverage, and for good reason. Gardner, from Chelmsford and only 15 years old at the time that he composed and performed the song, had created a work of remarkable maturity and arresting emotional expressiveness which ably articulated the effects of dementia not only on the individual who is fighting its symptoms, but also upon those who are close to them. While this topic may have been touched on by other musical artists in previous years, it was lent a sense of heightened immediacy when communicated by a teenager who was experiencing first-hand the far-reaching ways in which the condition was affecting his family.

Gardner felt compelled to embark upon the project due to his observations of the effects of Alzheimer's Disease upon his grandmother, Maureen McGuinness, then aged 76. Forced to retire from her checkout job at an Essex-based branch of a major national supermarket when she developed problems with numeracy, Maureen's mental health entered a period of sharp decline following her formal diagnosis of dementia. Becoming increasingly dependent upon the care provided by her husband Owen, the symptoms of her condition influenced Maureen in increasingly acute ways. She became distant and withdrawn, and during a family visit Gardner was startled and left shaken when he discovered that his once-sociable grandmother had now taken to separating herself from company, instead lying alone in darkness as though involuntarily removed from those around her. Though he had anticipated indications of the condition such as memory loss, Gardner was unprepared for the full effect that dementia would have upon his elderly relative, and the shock of the encounter galvanised him into expressing his complex melange of emotions into music and lyrics directly afterwards.

The song itself is both poignant and heartfelt, mourning his grandmother's inability to remember the experiences they shared together – and even her powerlessness to recognise Gardner himself. He also draws attention to the incongruity of the older woman's house having become quiet and despondent when she had always been a somewhat flamboyant individual, companionable and sociable prior to the onset of her condition. The rapidity of its progression, and her struggle against its effects, are motifs which are repeated throughout the song's lyrics.

One of the song's most arresting elements is Gardner's sincere and immediate regret over the way that dementia has impacted so overwhelmingly on Maureen's everyday living, meaning that even the subtlest things about their interactions have been disrupted. No longer can they watch television together, nor can she produce a bar of chocolate from her handbag as a treat for her grandson – her trademark gift. She has even been deprived of the ability to talk about the condition and voice regret about the way that it is affecting her life. Fear, anger, uncertainty... even these basic emotions are now beyond her ability to express, leading Gardner to reflect that no matter how his grandmother feels about her current circumstances, she has been cruelly divested of the capacity to convey her sentiments.

With an emotional maturity beyond his years, Gardner wishes for a reversal or nullification of his grandmother's symptoms while simultaneously acknowledging the fact that his yearnings are beyond the ability of current medical science to bring into being. The lyrics make clear his abstract sense of guilt that he should retain so many happy memories of times shared with Maureen when she has no way of recalling them for herself. Thus he contents himself with the fact that the responsibility now lies with him and his family to remember her as she was – the kindly, loving, matriarchal figure who brought so much to her family. This imperative seems all the more vital given the progressive deterioration that her mental faculties are undergoing as a result of Alzheimer's Disease.

There is no doubting the fact that 'Not Alone' is a song which is driven by deep love for a close relative and intense dejection as a result of their current situation, and yet the lyrics suggest even more innate and reflective aspects to Gardner's reaction to his grandmother's plight. There is a very real sense that he feels as though his own childhood has been invaded by the effects of Maureen's dementia; the good times that they spent together, where she would comment on how much he'd grown since she'd last seen him and always had time for a cup of tea and a chat, are now preserved only in the depths of his own memories, the reality having been wrested from him as he edges closer to adulthood. Thus we are left with the undeniable impression that the battle with dementia is a personal one in more ways than were perhaps immediately apparent – not only does Gardner have cause to feel resentment towards the disorder for the way in which it has so deleteriously affected his grandmother, but by highlighting the fact that his own fond memories of her have essentially been relegated to the past by the effects of the condition upon her neurology – thus underscoring the fact that her symptoms will only become more profound over time, even in spite of his desperate wish that she may recover – he clearly feels the indirect incursion of dementia's effects on his own early life, even though he is himself free from its physical and mental onset.

'Not Alone' contains considerable emotional nuance, and Gardner's powerful, unfussy piano accompaniment complements his lyrics in a suitably moving way without ever lingering on the distress of his feelings in a manner that is ever in danger of drifting into mawkishness or oversentimentality. The effect is commendably raw, mixing frustration over his inability to improve his grandmother's situation with a wistful regret over the realisation that the best times that he shared with Maureen have now been fated to drift into the past rather than remain in the present. It is a persuasive yet unobtrusive motif, encouraging each of us to value the time we spend with those who we are close to, as we never truly know how long these interactions will last.

A music video to accompany the song was filmed at Hylands House, a Grade II listed stately home situated in an historic parkland estate in Chelmsford, by director Kieran Hodges. (Though Gardner can be seen performing throughout the video, his grandmother was by this time too unwell to appear in person and was portrayed by an actress.) When released on YouTube it quickly accumulated views in the tens of thousands, attracting celebrity endorsement along the way. 'Not Alone' was also released on music streaming sites for purchase, with proceeds from the song being donated by Gardner to Alzheimer's Research UK in support of dementia support and research. While the positive outcomes of his creative and altruistic intentions – especially from someone of such a young age – were reported widely in the British media, much attention was also focused on the way in which the song had aided public understanding of the condition by focusing upon the way that the effects of dementia had so deeply affected Gardner and his family, as well as his grandmother herself.

Perhaps the most enduring legacy of 'Not Alone' was the way in which the song so perfectly summed up the feelings of confusion, anger, and pain suffered by someone who abhors the effects of dementia on a loved one, but who feels powerless to be able to aid them in combating these symptoms. Yet 'Not Alone' is never a song of defeat or regret, but rather one which exults in life, holding up treasured memories of a beloved relative almost as an act of defiance against the disease that had robbed her of her own recollections. In so poignantly celebrating the meaningfulness of the family unit and the affection that can span generations, Gardner's most conspicuous artistic achievement was not to lament that which dementia can steal from an individual, but rather to observe and applaud everything valuable about family ties and bonds of friendship that will always lie beyond its ability to reach.

13

RAGE AGAINST COMPLACENCY AND EXPECTATION

Whitechapel's 1, Dementia

WHILE the subject of dementia has lent itself to several thoughtful ballads in recent years, this is far from the only musical node to have been used to express feelings and opinions about the condition. Though the condition has often been dealt with in a manner which suggests a melancholic, almost resigned acceptance of an ever more alienating progression of its symptoms, other approaches instead reflect Dylan Thomas's oft-quoted desire to rage against the dying of the light; if the fight against the effects of dementia are so often depicted as a running battle, some musicians have made a conscious effort to express the contentious nature of the conflict in a deliberately more explicit manner within their work.

A leading light of the deathcore movement, Tennessee's Whitechapel have been fusing the genres of death metal and metalcore to considerable critical acclaim for more than a decade. Combining public popularity with an uncompromising and often graphic approach to heavyweight subject matter, the band has maintained notoriety through the release of well-received studio albums such as *This is Exile* (2008), *A New Era of Corruption* (2010), *Our Endless War* (2014), and *Mark of the Blade* (2016). (The band, which consists of vocalist Phil Bozeman, bassist Gabe Crisp, and guitarists Zach Householder, Ben Savage, and Alex Wade, took its name from the district of London which infamously played host to the still-unsolved Jack the Ripper murders in 1888.) With a musical focus that has ranged from the emotional intensity of graphic horror and psychological extremes of differing types of violence, it may have come as something of a surprise that they would also use their work to explore the manifold effects of dementia on the human psychology – and in the least predictable of ways.

Written by Alex Wade, Phil Bozeman and Ben Savage, 'I, Dementia' is the fourth track on *Whitechapel*, the band's self-titled fourth studio album which was released in June 2012 through the Metal Blade Records label. (A music video, directed by David Brodsky and paying skilful visual tribute to the style of the White Stripes' 'Seven Nation Army', was released shortly before the album hit the market.) While the song may be a typically intense and heartfelt number, retaining more than a trace of the band's characteristic groove metal roots, its provocative lyrics articulate an exploration of dementia which is as stimulating as it is exigent.

Perhaps the most immediately arresting aspect of 'I, Dementia' is the band's personification of the condition as both destructive and capricious. For Whitechapel, we quickly realise, dementia is not the vexatious robber of memory so prominently conveyed in many avenues of popular culture, but rather an aggressive and obdurate attacker, assailing the individual's sense of self and perception of reality with equal violence. Here, we see the disorder cast not in its customary role as a gradual, inexorably advancing cause of impairment, but rather as a brutal and even sadistic force – malign in intention and destructive in action – as it mockingly taunts the individual who is affected by it.

Whitechapel are well known for their no-holds-barred approach, and 'I, Dementia' is no exception; strong language and stark imagery are used, albeit only when necessary, to illustrate not just the impact of dementia but also the impotent fury of the person who is fighting the condition. The individual is not passive, but finds that retaliation is impossible. How, they quite reasonably ask, can they rail against something so intangible that it cannot even be reliably defined? We become aware that this is not simply a medical condition to be diagnosed and treated, but a belligerent, ethereal aggressor which cannot be reasoned with or assuaged.

As the song continues, it becomes more evident that the boundaries between reality and delusion are being blurred, or even erased altogether. A bleak note

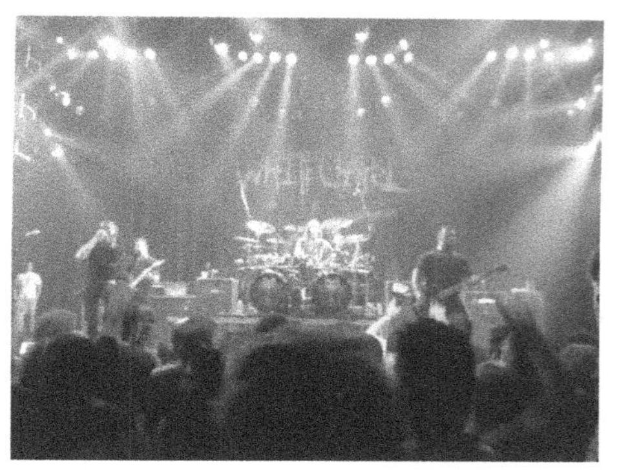

Whitechapel

permeates the narrative as the person with the condition desperately seeks escape from their situation, but knows that their own existence has become inextricably interlinked with that of the disorder. Their life has become so deeply affected by the onset of dementia that they find it impossible to extricate their personal sense of self from the tendrils of the condition which have insidiously snaked into every aspect of their being.

There is, of course, a strong indication – particularly evident in the song's closing line – that the dementia we have heard discussed is not just the medical condition, but a wider sense of postmodern (perhaps even post-postmodern) malaise which is so often accused of undermining society's shared experience of 'authentic' reality and replacing it with a kind of relativism which cannot be consistently defined or relied upon. This duality of purpose is adroitly underplayed. We see dementia depicted not only in terms of distorting or destroying a sense of normality, but also in its capacity to obfuscate the individual's grasp of what provides a reliable basis of comparison where existential veracity is concerned: this may be true of society and culture as much as it is in terms of psychological and sensory familiarity. But as had been the case in their examination of the disorder based in terms of a particularised entity, no straightforward answers are ever posited.

Perhaps the most laudable aspect of 'I, Dementia' is Whitechapel's absolute refusal to attempt to impose easy answers to the conflict that they are depicting. Just as there are no straightforward parameters to the war which is being fought from opposing positions between polarities – reality and illusion, reason and illogicality, order and chaos – so too are we guided to understand that identifying a comfortable compromise will always be impossible. As the lyrics make clear, dementia is not simply a condition which confronts the status quo and seeks to destabilise it; instead, the disorder irrevocably changes the terms upon which people live, reshaping not just their lives but also their sense of self-identification. It is this obdurate capacity of dementia to deconstruct not just an individual's perception of the world around them, but also ultimately reshaping and redefining the coherence of their personal mindset, which appears to be the factor that troubles Whitechapel the most.

There is genuine anger to be found in 'I, Dementia', and it is focused primarily upon the song's essential impulse towards compelling the listener to assert their individuality and revel in their autonomy as forcefully as possible, and for as long as possible. There is subtle correlation drawn throughout the song between a modern society that essentially thrives upon conformity to achieve its goals – cultural forces shaping autonomous human beings to stringently correspond to particular roles and duties in order to accomplish specific goals, even if their endpoint is not necessary advantageous to the worker themselves – and the capacity of dementia to unwillingly transform individuals into an unrecognisable version of their personal selves that has been slowly stripped of memory, of independence, and of reliable perception. But this social criticism, though barbed in nature, is almost superfluous to the elemental conflict that the song describes. The central theme is inevitably one of oppression: where a force that gradually divests someone of the ability to recognise loved ones, distinguish the passage of time, or even identify their whereabouts, is cast in the role of an indistinctly-defined persecutor. The audience is encouraged to sympathise with the plight of those labouring under the tyranny of such subjugation, because they themselves may well be in just as much danger from its onset.

'I, Dementia' is a challenging song, but one which exhibits a multi-faceted strategy to flesh out a complex and often misunderstood condition. Through repetition of – and unanticipated deviation from – its key motifs of disorientation and perceptual deception, a desolate image is constructed of a prolonged struggle against an relentless and illusive tormentor: a battle which appears to have only one possible outcome. In the style of much of their work, Whitechapel do not attempt to sugar-coat the progression and behaviour of a pernicious condition, and certainly no endeavour is made to impose an unrealistically upbeat conclusion to the devastating conflict depicted throughout the song. But by this same token, 'I,

Dementia' is more than the sum of its parts, ultimately transcending what may otherwise have been a nihilistic and rather austere exercise in hopelessness. For this is a song which is more concerned with expressing a need for greater mutual understanding than in voicing timeworn clichés, drawing a nexus of commonality between individuals and societies by charting the march of a condition which is universal both in its reach and its effects. And though it may prove to be demanding listening for many, not least in its strident and unwavering methodology, the song seems most concerned with valuing the life of the individual, lamenting isolation and societal indifference just as much as it emphasises the detrimental effects of dementia itself.

14

CELEBRATING SUPERHEROES OF THE EVERYDAY

Massive Dog's When You Were Superman

INTERGENERATIONAL attitudes towards dementia have become an issue of increasing interest as crucial educational campaigns continue to inform the public of the issues surrounding the condition, emphasising that it can – and actively does – affect people of all ages and from all walks of life, meaning that more must be done to support those who are affected. The universality of the condition has been touched upon in various creative approaches, though its impact on lives both young and old is one which bears greater consideration. Music is an excellent discipline to engender awareness of the issues surrounding dementia and the ways that it affects family members across generations, and this very topic became the subject of a well-received song written and performed by Colin and Dan Parish, otherwise known as indie band Massive Dog.

Released in September 2014, 'When You Were Superman' was distributed through a number of popular digital music outlets, and the band made a donation from every sale to the Alzheimer's Society, making clear their intention that their music was intended not only to inform audiences of this important concern, but also to have a tangible benefit for an organisation which supports people who are affected by the disorder as well as being deeply involved with constant research into the disease.

With its strikingly understated instrumentation and distinctively genuine, heartfelt vocals, 'When You Were Superman' immediately arrests the audience with its no-nonsense approach to what is, for many people, an abstruse subject to engage with. The narrator discusses the respect and even awe that he holds for his father, who – we are told – was always a larger-than-life character with a resourceful manner and strong family values. Such is the love and admiration that he has holds for his father, in fact, that he compares him throughout the song with D.C. Comics's world-famous Superman, Jerry Siegel and Joe Schuster's instantly-recognisable comic book character who has become synonymous with the superhero genre since his first appearance in 1933.

Because Superman is arguably the most readily identifiable superhero in all of graphic fiction, the contrasts which are struck by the song become all the more poignant. The narrator's father is depicted as an inventive and practical man who always seemed to hold all the answers; someone who approached life with indomitable good humour and optimism, even though he had personally faced the horrors of war as a young man. But as times change, so too can circumstances. As the narrator himself becomes a father, discovering the joys and the responsibilities of parenthood, he draws a painful juxtaposition between his son's growing skills and his own father's declining abilities as a result of dementia's onset. Just as the narrator's son learns to tie his shoelaces, for instance, we are told that his father has lost the aptitude to tie his own. For a man whose creativity and strength of character had made him a legend in the eyes of his family, this erosion of capacity is especially difficult to come to terms with.

Yet for all the moving sincerity of its central topic, 'When You Were Superman' is not a song to descend headlong into overt sentimentality. Though the narrator's father is declining as a result of the dementia which is affecting his abilities, and is intermittently aware of the effects of the condition as it continues to progress, he retains his stoicism and playful light-heartedness even as his family witness his personal deterioration. But as his father's memories fade and his practical skills gradually wane, the narrator laments the fact that he has no way of locating and removing Kryptonite (the fictional, extraterrestrial substance which robbed Superman of his powers whenever he came into contact with it), and thus has no way of ridding his father of the difficulties which are afflicting him. However, he knows only too well that dementia is no comic book phenomenon, and recognises that in the real world no superpowers or *deus ex machina* conclusion will suddenly come to light in order to lessen its effects.

Written by Colin Parish as he witnessed his father Sidney's cognitive decline as a result of dementia, the song was later developed in collaboration with Colin's nephew Dan Parish, who reworked the music beyond its initial ukulele-based iteration into its current format. With its unwavering tone of earnestness and a genuine willingness to tackle the issues which face families when dealing with dementia, the song forms a dignified and well-meaning attempt to highlight the ways in which the condition affects not just the person who is diagnosed with it, but also everyone who is close to that individual. The audience knows, just as the narrator does, that while the father in this song is being compared to a cape-wearing hero in possession of extraordinary physical strength and mental agility, he is ultimately just a human being like anyone else – but such is his stature amongst his family, to them he appears to be so much more than that. Yes, he is undoubtedly unique... but – we are reminded – in their own way, so is everyone. And so it is with friends and families across the world; every person has the potential to appear extraordinary to those around them, and similarly they are all equally at risk from the onset of dementia or will know or care for someone who is affected by it at some point in their lives.

One of the most successful aspects of the song is the way in which Parish combines the fantastical with the commonplace. His father is likened to a superhero, but we know that every son and daughter who share a good relationship with their parent may well look on them with the same affection. Suddenly, this paterfamilias – who had always been the practical figure who seemed to have a solution for almost every problem – finds himself forced to deal with a condition that defies his ability to overcome it. No matter how hard he may try, there is no solution to be found to resist this new menace; unlike a comic book threat that can be combated, usually through teamwork and/or quick thinking at the last minute, dementia proves to be a threat too aggressive and pervasive to resolve effectively. Thus this cheerfully pragmatic man, who has survived bloody conflict and any number of life difficulties in his time, gradually finds that his extensive skills and abilities are not enough to turn back the tide of a danger that even medical science cannot deal with.

Key to 'When You Were Superman' is the power of emotional bonds, and their capacity to ameliorate even that which superpowers cannot overcome. Dementia's effects may prove that the narrator's father is not invincible, but this realisation and its subsequent developments ultimately do nothing to diminish him in the eyes of his family and friends. Though they find it difficult to face the unpalatable truth that this supremely capable, well-loved figure is not invulnerable after all, their affection and respect for him remain undimmed. And while such love may not be able to reverse the symptoms of dementia, it ensures that those who are close to the song's central figure will remember him as the exuberant, capable individual that they had always known, rather than allowing the progression of his condition to fog their recognition of his distinctiveness. With great, understated power, the song reminds us of the need to value those close to us at all times, for we never know when their health may fail, their mental faculties may falter, or they may be taken from us unexpectedly.

An animated music video to accompany the song, produced in collaboration with CreativeConnection, was made available on YouTube and quickly garnered thousands of views. The video was to further increase the song's visibility at the time of release, and was a highly inventive combination of hand-drawn art and stop-motion animation. This allowed a highly effective approach which added a sense of movement to imagery that would otherwise have been static, while the addition of a red scarf – which is associated with the father figure throughout the video – is used as a motif to chart the advancement of the condition on the character's life. Eventually it becomes a more universal image, with identical red scarves being worn by a group of the same man's friends and family at the end of the video as they pay homage to a life lived fruitfully – emphasising not only the way in which they value his memory, but also the fact that his condition could potentially effect each and every one of them in turn.

Because of the song's emphasis on intergenerational relations and the universality of dementia as a condition which has the ability to touch every life in one way or another, Massive Dog produced a work with surprisingly expressive power and emotional subtlety – all the more effective for its sensitivity and unexpected persuasiveness. The work is as memorable as it is engaging, and in its readiness to address the collective commonality of a condition which is still too often stigmatised or confronted by indirect means it must be commended for its veracity and creditable forthrightness.

15

TRUE EMOTION AND NEBULOUS PERCEPTION

Chadwick Johnson's *Remember Love*

DEMENTIA is a condition so multifaceted, and with implications that are so comprehensive, that music which features it has drawn from many different traditions and creative inspirations in an attempt to articulate the consequences that a diagnosis has for individuals affected by the disease, those close to them, and indeed for society in general. With his song 'Remember Love', award-winning recording artist and songwriter Chadwick Johnson made a praiseworthy attempt to capture the treasured experiences spent with friends and family members who are affected by dementia, overcoming obstacles such as disorientation and failure of memory to appreciate the immediate present. For

Johnson, memories of the past may be cherished but will eventually become inaccessible for the person affected by dementia, whereas worrying about the future is a fruitless endeavour due to the fact that dwelling on the condition's progression will do nothing to stop its encroachment upon everyday life. Instead, he stresses the need to make the most of every moment of every day – to recognise the fact that every life is a tapestry woven from a plethora of invaluable moments.

Wisconsin-born Chadwick Johnson has become a well-respected name in the music industry of the United States, winning the Male Vocalist of the Year Award at the 2015 Hollywood Music in Media Awards. Particularly well-known for his appearances on the Las Vegas Strip, he has performed in many different venues across the world, as well as having taken part in a command performance for US President Bill Clinton.

His music having achieved considerable popularity via online streaming sites, Johnson's visibility as an artist was to reach new heights in 2016 with the release of 'Remember Love', a song which explored the effects of dementia from the personal viewpoint of someone close to the individual who is battling the condition. Written by Johnson in collaboration with songwriter Kalani Queypo, Johnson performed the vocals for 'Remember Love' with the song's guitar arrangement and performance contributed by Tasos Peltekis. Proceeds from the sale of the song were donated to the Cleveland Clinic Lou Ruvo Center for Brain Health, with the intention of aiding their work in treating the symptoms of dementia and eventually finding a cure for the condition.

Johnson is an artist who delivers meticulous and polished performances, and this was never more true than in the case of 'Remember Love'. Lending his versatile vocal talents to the delivery of moving and powerful lyrics, he provides the song with an admirable level of unaffectedness. A charismatic and compelling stage presence, there is no doubting Johnson's commitment to the principle that music exhibits an incredible capacity to resonate with people who have dementia, reaching them in ways that many other more conventional means of communication are unable to. He and his co-writer Queypo have discussed in interviews the importance of music as a kind of universal means of interaction, helping to convey positive emotions and comforting sentiments to individuals affected by dementia, and both men have stressed the importance of appreciating the needs of not only those who have been diagnosed with the illness, but also providing whatever reassurance is possible for their loved ones who are also struggling with the effects that dementia is having on their family member, friend, or acquaintance.

With a haunting but restrained vocal, Johnson's approach to the performance of 'Remember Love' is one of unobtrusive power and reflective contemplation. The song concerns the protagonist's concerns for a close acquaintance – presumably a close relative, or a long-time companion – who is now facing the onset of dementia and its inexorable advancement. Throughout the narrative, the aching damage of memory loss is very much brought to the forefront of the song's concerns; not only on account of the day-to-day issues that are caused by lack of recall, but also due to the fact that the relationships of the person with dementia are being impaired by the fact that they are no longer able to effectively remember even those who are close to them. There is an undeniable emphasis on the fact that dementia is not simply a collection of symptoms that bear down upon the mental faculties of a person who is affected by it, but also a far-reaching and destructive phenomenon which erodes not just their psychiatric capacity but also many of the qualities which characterise their individual self.

The song's narrator is only too painfully aware of the corrosion acting upon the autonomy and personal self-identification of their loved one, and thus he calls to mind not the need to remember for the sake of reconstructing personal identity – which he knows is now beyond their own capabilities to rectify – but rather the necessity to love and be loved, which is an emotional response that transcends the logic and rationality being gradually worn away by the progression of dementia. It is this shared devotion and camaraderie which, Johnson and Queypo's lyrics highlight, have the aptitude to ensure that the bonds of friendship and familial love can continue uninterrupted when the usual modes of interpersonal communication have long since become disturbed and corrupted.

The song employs strong elemental symbolism of light breaking through darkness, signifying love and friendship shining like a beacon as it overcomes the mental miasma caused by dementia. But the same sentiment is also conveyed by less anticipated means; the narrator at one point asserts their intention to become not just a light in the darkness for the person affected by dementia, but also their steady breath when health fails them; the rhythm of sound and song, when all else has gone silent. This simple but highly effective declaration of the underlying strength of interpersonal friendship and familial love carries such potency simply because of its straightforwardness. It is clear that the narrator cannot imagine life without their loved one, to the point that they are willing to perform any means of personal support in order to ease the difficulties of their ever-increasing malady. He is fully aware that the battle will only get harder for both of the song's key figures, and yet he is nonetheless willing to defy this inevitability because his affection for the person with dementia far outweighs the manifest difficulties involved in providing such care.

'Remember Love' also proves highly effectual in its use of time as a complex motif. The listener is made fully aware of the fact that time, which is so often cast in the role of the great healer, is instead pitilessly subverted into the function of a malign influence – one which is ushering in ever-greater difficulty as a result of dementia's progressive effects on the person affected by it. Yet conversely, the tendency of dementia to disrupt the concept of time's passage is also explored; the condition dislocates the conception of time as a universal invariant, demonstrating the ways in which a person battling dementia may suffer from impaired perception that makes chronological advancement far from a linear process. Events from the far-flung past may at times appear much more immediate than they should, whereas other experiences may be lost altogether as the result of compromised recall of fractured memories. The song deals with this multifarious issue in commendably eloquent ways, ensuring that the complication of this dense and wide-ranging subject is never underplayed while simultaneously communicating its implications with both elegance and earnestness.

The creative aims and charitable objectives of 'Remember Love' were widely publicised at the time of the song's release in 2016, with Johnson appearing in video and print interviews to promote the song as well as penning original articles about the artistic intentions behind his music. He later gave a recital of 'Remember Love' as part of a two performance, one night only event which took place at Cabaret Jazz at the famous Smith Center in Las Vegas, with proceeds from ticket sales donated to dementia research, and the song was also to feature prominently on his successful 2017 album *Live in Las Vegas*. It is easy to see why 'Remember Love' has become one of his best-regarded works, for it deals with the problematic effects of dementia in ways which bring emotional immediacy and personal warmth to a subject that is, all too often, regarded in starkly clinical terms. While it is tempting to be most impressed – from a critical standpoint – with the lyrics' unbending determination to engage with sometimes thorny conceptual apparatus to delineate difficult emotions surrounding an even more problematic subject, at its heart 'Remember Love' is a work about mutual understanding, and finding shared commonality in the face of adversity. For at the core of the song is a common humanity, imploring the listener to never forget the fact that everyone affected by dementia is a human being who deserves dignity, respect and understanding.

16

A EUPHORIC CHALLENGE TO DELIRIUM

Owl City's Dementia

FEW people could have turned on their radio in the summer of 2008 without hearing the sound of Owl City's famous song 'Fireflies'. The ubiquitous synth-pop single topped the charts around the world, including in the UK and USA, and eventually led to six-time platinum bestselling status. Brainchild of singer-songwriter Adam Young, an acclaimed Minnesotan multi-instrumentalist, Owl City's distinctive brand of electronica has continued to win many fans across the world since the project burst onto the scene in 2007. After the success of the independently-produced album *Maybe I'm Dreaming* in 2008, mainstream triumph accompanied the release of *Ocean Eyes* (2009) and *All Things Bright and Beautiful* (2010), which ensured that the band has remained comfortably in the public eye ever since. Later albums, such as *Mobile Orchestra* (2015) and *Cinematic* (2018), have only helped to cement Young's reputation as an artist of flair and creative diversity.

It was in 2012 with the release of Owl City's fourth album, *The Midsummer Station*, that Young was to address the topic of dementia. Penned by Young himself, the track (entitled simply 'Dementia') was to explore the subject in a typically thought-provoking and off-kilter manner; as the band had already covered themes as varied as insomnia, environmental pollution and even the *Challenger* Space Shuttle disaster, the issue of mental illness – a phenomenon which affects a large and growing percentage of society across the globe – certainly could not be considered a topic too far from the beaten track for a group which had already established a critical reputation for deftly subverting artistic expectation. The song also featured a collaboration with producer and Blink-182 member Mark Hoppus, who provided its distinctive lead vocal.

Like much of Owl City's output, Young's song is open to multiple interpretations. Although the word 'dementia' is featured regularly throughout the song's lyrics (fifteen times within a three-and-a-half minute duration), as well as forming the title itself, the listener quickly discovers that they are not by any means witnessing a conventional assessment of the condition. For Young, dementia proves to be the end result of a pitched battle between euphoria and delirium, causing restlessness, confusion, and disorientation. There is, of course, nothing remotely euphoric about the condition itself –

quite the opposite, in fact. So what does his song posit as being the cause of these symptoms? Here, various analyses are possible.

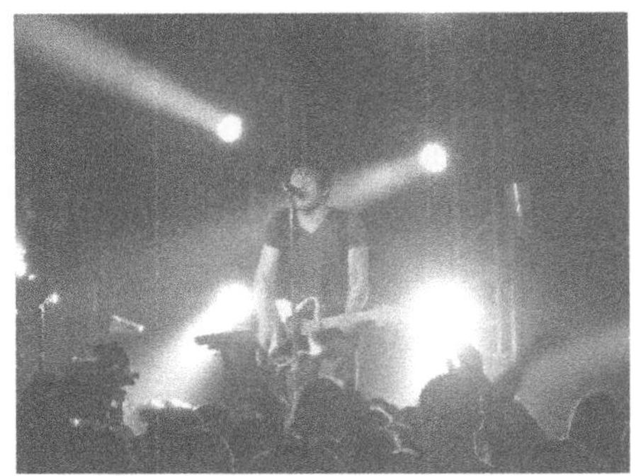

Adam Young

At face value, the song appears to depict a protagonist who is disappointed and aggrieved after repeated romantic rejection. Finding a new love interest, this enigmatic figure discovers that they are afraid to declare their feelings to the other party, leading to an emotional tug of war where the exhilaration of new romance is thwarted by fear of being rebuffed, leading to the protagonist being engulfed by competing emotions as they watch their intended partner from afar. Young explicitly describes this emotional tension as a conflict between passion and (self-)hostility, becoming so intense that it ultimately results in a kind of psychosis. But in spite of what the song would have us believe, this type of emotive discord does not – of course – describe dementia or its symptoms in a way that would be recognised in any clinical interpretation. And as Young does not have a tendency to treat such matters either trivially or disrespectfully within his music, an additional reading of the song appears necessary to provide the full picture.

Because the central premise of the song is psychological conflict – between love and hate, lucidity and irrationality, self-esteem and self-loathing – it may be conceived that the entirety of 'Dementia' is, in fact, a lyrical examination not of experiences which mimic the illness, but of the symptoms of the condition themselves. The frustration of the protagonist, whose aggravated dissatisfaction superficially appears motivated by an impeded declaration of love, may also be explained by an allusion towards personal rejection in the face of public misunderstanding of dementia, its causes, and its effects. The lyrics speak of delusionary phenomena, of emotional confusion, and of personal isolation – all aspects of the condition which are much more relevant, and more plausible, than the notion of the dementia-like symptoms being stimulated in a manner as described in the previous interpretation. In this reading of the song, Young appears to be making a plea for greater awareness of dementia, to broaden comprehension in a way that will increase public support and thus decrease the kind of loneliness and seclusion that the protagonist so affectingly describes.

Though songs dealing with dementia are far from plentiful, the strategy of employing polar opposites to express the condition's effects has become a fairly common approach. Thus the conflict between reality and delusion is mirrored throughout the song in the juxtaposition which Young posits between light and dark, hot and cold, order and chaos. Then, of course, the listener is presented with further interpolation of the depiction of dementia's encroachment into the lives of those affected by it (the incursion of disorder into regularity), which subsumes the initial scenario of the unbearable intensity of emotions which roils around the exhilaration of new love and the anxiety of rejection (contentment in conflict with unease). Every level of the song, it seems, is based upon polarity, very effectively using binary opposition to convey its central theme of immutable variance.

As might be expected from such a thematic stratagem, there are no straightforward answers to be posited; Young conceives the very concept of dementia to be an agent of disarray and confusion, unable to be appeased by any countering phenomenon. Thus the situation he postulates is less a case of an unmovable object meeting an irresistible force, but rather that of a relentless power which throws all that it encounters into turmoil. This may seem like a rather bleak assessment, blunted as it is by the outer narrative's deliberately deceptive evocation of transitory attraction and possibly-thwarted romance, but Young's determination to depict dementia as a kind of elemental force which knows neither mercy nor reason is a deeply effective one which articulates the devastation caused by the disease in an admirably uncompromising way.

While it is true that this multi-layered interpretation of the song does admittedly make it seem like a rather more stark listening experience than its ostensibly off-the-cuff romantic narrative may suggest, there is little doubting the incisive power of Young's lyrics – delivered with characteristic gusto by Hoppus. If the accompanying tale of starry-eyed insecurity is perceived as an attempt to sugar-coat an otherwise difficult subject, this notion is cleanly disavowed by the asceticism of the song's austere, unambiguous use of repeated opposites to make its point about the regrettable but unrelenting march of dementia's progression once its onset takes hold. While at face value the contrast of contrary phenomena may suggest that dementia can somehow be frustrated or neutralised, the repetition instead suggests the contrary: that no matter which force emerges to counter its advancement, the end result is unavoidable. Yet rather than simply introducing this desolate reading of the situation for the sake of realism, Young may also be making a plea to his audience to show greater understanding towards people who are affected by dementia, underscoring the discouraging fight that they face against an implacable disorder. By that same token, his depiction of the disease as being essentially overwhelming in nature may also be interpreted as a rallying cry; an entreaty for human ingenuity – through scientific research and medical technology – to tame and eradicate that which has proven to be personally devastating and thus far uncontrollable.

It is entirely a matter of personal opinion whether 'Dementia' employs the condition as a poetic device, an allegory for extreme emotional upset which defies the accepted medical narrative, or rather harnesses it in a way which has the goal of encouraging greater consideration of the disorder. As is so often the way with Young's song-writing, the listener is persuaded to draw their own conclusions from the evidence which is presented. Certainly the material is dense enough for more than one analysis to be drawn, but one fact does appear to remain prominent beyond all others: that Young intends to make his audience aware that dementia is a condition which has far-reaching effects upon the person who is experiencing it, as well as those who are around them, and that greater understanding is essential to counter stigma and inspire acceptance – something that is just as essential as fighting the disease itself.

Dramatic and Performance Arts

17

AN OPERATIC ARTICULATION OF DEMENTIA

John O' Hara and Karen Hayes's The Bargee's Wife

OF all performance styles, opera has always had a matchless capacity amongst musical art-forms for channelling raw emotion. It is an artistic medium whose palette offers a powerful blend of intensity and sensitivity which has captivated audiences for centuries. Ranging from the work of Mozart to Verdi to Rossetti, opera has presented timeless accounts of ill-fated romance and struggles for authority, where comedy and tragedy rub shoulders in ways unmatched by so many other modes of creative expression. It seems of little surprise, given opera's consummate ability to impart emotional complexity and hard-hitting subject matter, that in recent years the form has been used to explore dementia and its manifold effects upon those who are affected by the condition.

The Bargee's Wife is a community opera which was created in collaboration between composer John O'Hara and poet and librettist Karen Hayes. Debuting in August 2013 as part of the Three Choirs Festival with a gala performance at Gloucester Cathedral, conducted by O'Hara himself, the performance was headlined by popular musical talent Barbara Dickson and featured an admirably nuanced narrative which expended every effort in investigating the far-reaching ramifications of dementia upon memory and self-awareness. Set during the extreme winter of 1963, the opera takes place on the Sharpness and Severn Canal where a sudden unexpected tragedy sends shockwaves throughout the boating community. This misfortune – and the heartbreak that it brings – resonates down through the generations, and is remembered in markedly different ways by a group of witnesses to the event in the present day. However, as these narrators are each affected by dementia (albeit in subtly different ways), the exact details of their testimonies are not always in harmony.

Although John O'Hara has perhaps been best-known within popular culture as an accordionist and pianist/Hammond organist for rock band Jethro Tull, this Royal Northern College of Music graduate has excelled as a lecturer and composer, being responsible for operatic works and the musical scores of stage dramas scores which have been performed by the Washington National Orchestra, the Royal Liverpool Philharmonic Orchestra, the Rambert Dance Company, and the National Theatre, amongst several others. He also served as the resident musical director and composer at the Bristol Old Vic for many years. Karen Hayes has specialised in working with people who have been diagnosed with dementia, and has written numerous poetic works (including anthologies such as *Only Just Orchid*, 2007, and *The Edges of Everywhere*, 2007) which have used as their focus the voices of individuals who encounter difficulty being heard or recognised. The immense importance of personal identity, and means of articulating it even through a fog of confusion and uncertainty, is often core to her work.

Building upon this extensive professional experience of the subject area, Hayes and composer John O'Hara worked with a number of people in their eighties and nineties – all of whom had been diagnosed with dementia – in order to ascertain their various personal accounts of life working in and around the canal. Collaborating with the Mindsong charity, they collectively acted to ensure that the voices of people with dementia were fully respected and accurately documented. Once this had been achieved, the recollections and feelings of these individuals were painstakingly crafted into the cohesive operatic work which became *The Bargee's Wife* in order to guarantee the maximum level of historical authenticity.

During the performance, the disparate reminiscences about the canal are expressed using three separate soloists – each with the somewhat nebulous names of

'Then', 'Soon', and 'Now'. These characters express different aspects of shared life experiences, while simultaneously reflecting the disparity which exists between nostalgia for the past, uncertainty about the present, and apprehension regarding the future. Crucial to the events of the opera is the eponymous bargee's wife herself, a figure who is lent an ethereal sense of otherworldliness due to her presence both as a memory of bygone times and a manifestation of emotional ambiguity.

While the 'action' of the opera is evoked through lyrical means, the emotive nature of the central incident which drives the narrative – the death by drowning of a young girl in the canal during the 1930s – ensures that the resulting chronicle of events could not fail to be poignant and affecting. The nimble alternation between past, present, and future led more than one critic to draw comparisons to the work of T.S. Eliot, and yet Hayes's dialogic strategy manages to carve its own niche; here we are led not only to question the reliability of memory after so many years have passed, but also to consider the effects of dementia on the accuracy of the particular account that is being portrayed. Accompanied by O'Hara's heart-rending music, which effortlessly fluctuates between wistfulness and immediacy as necessary, a disconnected and sometimes contradictory account eventually emerges of the young girl's fate, and the audience becomes aware of the heightened degree of emotional distress which still accompanies these long-bygone events in a way which resonates not just into the present, but also continues to remain raw for times yet to come.

In its praiseworthy attempt to delineate the unreliability of personal narrative and the fragmented nature of individual identity, *The Bargee's Wife* skilfully recalls the strategies of Ryunosuke Akutagawa's early modernist short story *In a Grove* (1922), later adapted to great acclaim by Akira Kurosawa in the form of his cinematic masterpiece *Rashōmon* (1950). Events are hazily demarcated, their accuracy dimmed by the passing of time and the shifting of viewpoints which make specific memories impossible to circumscribe with either reliability or anything approaching precision. The audience are encouraged to make up their own minds regarding this indeterminate account of past events, and are left to draw their conclusions from the complex emotional tapestry of wistfulness and foreboding which is presented to them.

While the death of an innocent cannot fail to be emotionally devastating, thus ensuring that the central premise of the young girl's drowning remains a constantly compelling issue throughout the opera, it seems particularly interesting that – for much of *The Bargee's Wife* – audience attention is focused not simply on resolving the mortality as though it were some kind of mystery, but rather in exploring the devastation that the event had on the community who populated the canal at the time. Dementia may have dimmed the ability of those who witnessed the tragedy to exactly recall the details of what had happened, but the sense of heartbreak and shared grief remains undiminished by the passing of time. O'Hara's otherworldly shift between choral and folk music only aids in emphasising the honesty of the accounts as they emerge from the shadows of years past; ultimately the audience learns more about the ways that dementia can affect identity and remembrance than it ascertains about hard facts surrounding the central death that nominally drives the opera's narrative.

The involvement of Mindsong – and the organisation's expertise in music therapy – in aiding in the sourcing of the core accounts relating to the central tragedy from witnesses aids in the unwavering authenticity of the voices which are heard throughout *The Bargee's Wife*, ensuring that all contributing accounts are faithfully respected while never attempting to claim that the end result is either factually cohesive or entirely reliable in terms of verifiable accuracy. And it is precisely because of the way in which dementia is recognised as an agent of misperception and uncertainty in relating the events of yesteryear that the narrative is lent such devastating power; the accidental death of an innocent child may be chalked up by some as merely a tragic footnote in local history, but – for those who witnessed it – it remains a tender, visceral, and emotional experience which has retained its impact on individuals and the community long after the material facts of the accident have faded into obscurity.

O'Hara and Hayes's opera is a challenging but rewarding experience, the soloists supported by the musical talents of two separate choruses (one composed of a 160-strong host of adults, the other a demi-chorus of child singers) to powerful effect. The overall impact is as commanding as it is disconcerting, the intentional lack of narrative clarity or chronological lucidity combining to subordinate logical certainty to the unpredictable currents of emotional feeling. *The Bargee's Wife* is a powerful example of the ability of musical performance to formulate mood and sentiment through potent but unconventional methods, heightening emotive awareness while concurrently expressing the fleeting nature of personal experience. It is, to date, one of the most original operatic compositions to draw upon dementia as its focal subject, and remains estimable in its respect for the voices of those affected by the condition as well as its determination not to impose a fallacious sense of orderliness upon the intricate network of individual memories and personal pronouncements that it weaves.

18

MISPLACED PROPERTY AND RECOLLECTIONS

Ian Kershaw's Lost and Found

GIVEN the increasing availability of TV and film material across the world, whether delivered to mobile devices or streamed across the Internet, it remains a comfort to know that audio drama remains a popular and uniquely flexible medium which has retained the ability to reach mass audiences around the world. The popularity of specialist full-cast audio drama producers such as Audible and Big Finish Productions, and the ready accessibility of Internet-based archives from the golden age of the format – featuring such acting greats as Orson Welles and James Stewart, amongst many others – have combined to keep this highly distinctive mode of performance firmly in the public eye. While recordings from the golden age of radio are often used for purposes of reminiscence, helping older people affected by dementia to reconnect with their youth, the audio drama format has just as important a part to play in the here and now when it comes to identifying issues which derive from dementia and encouraging greater understanding of the condition.

With its reliance upon the power of the spoken word and the vocal acting talents of their respective casts, radio dramas remain one of the BBC's most popular broadcast features over the airwaves, and throughout the years productions have readily engaged with many issues of political, social, and cultural import. Dementia – and the complex ethical and philosophical issues which are related to the condition – has been no exception, and in recent years the BBC has typically engaged with this multifaceted subject with much creative integrity, confronting misconceptions and confronting audience apathy towards this problematic mental illness.

Perhaps most prominent amongst the Corporation's dementia-related features since the turn of the decade has been *Lost and Found*, a radio play first broadcast on the afternoon of Monday 2nd December 2013 to much critical approval. Directed and produced by Gary Brown, the play was written by Ian Kershaw – a highly experienced screenwriter, whose output has thus far encompassed everything from episodes of popular TV series such as *EastEnders*, *Casualty* and *Shameless* through to the 2014 Gillies MacKinnon-helmed drama *Castles in the Sky* (a well-received biopic of radar pioneer Robert

Watson-Watt, starring Eddie Izzard) and the emotionally intense short film *Room 42* (2012). Winner of a Bronze Award for Best Drama at the 2014 Radio Academy Awards, *Lost and Found* takes full advantage of the audio-only performance format to raise intriguing questions about the malleability of identity and the ability of people to psychologically and emotionally connect with one another on multiple levels.

The year is 1979, shortly after the landslide victory of Margaret Thatcher's Conservative Party. Public servant Stan (Tom Courtenay) is hard at work in a lost property office, which he operates within a busy railway station in the heart of Manchester. Interrupting the monotony of his day, a woman in her mid-forties named Zoe (Sally Carman) arrives at the office in search of something that she claims to have lost. As an individual who takes great pride in his job, Stan gladly offers his assistance in tracking down the elusive item. As their professional interaction continues, however, it soon becomes apparent that all is not quite as it seems. For as events progress, the listener discovers that Stan is not in fact a 1970s public sector employee at all, but rather an elderly gentleman living in a modern-day care home, whereas his mysterious visitor actually transpires to be his own daughter. Thus as the play draws towards its conclusion, the audience becomes aware that the whole imaginative construct of the lost property office is in fact a device by which parent and child alike must engage with their shared experiences as a way of relating to each other.

Kershaw's deeply moving script, which never trivialises its subject matter nor allows the action to stray into maudlin sentimentality, is skilfully brought to life by long-time performance veteran Sir Tom Courtenay – an Academy Award-nominated actor immediately recognisable to filmgoers as the protagonist of John Schlesinger's *Billy Liar* (1963) and as Pasha in David Lean's famous Boris Pasternak adaptation *Doctor Zhivago* (1965), though perhaps better known to younger audiences as Lance Corporal Jack Jones (a role originally made famous by Clive Dunn) in Oliver Parker's 2016 cinematic remake of the BBC's *Dad's Army*. With an expansive career in the entertainment industry which has included appearances on television, cinema and the stage, Courtenay's authoritative tones seem tailor-made for radio, and yet it is his performance's tightly-controlled articulation of melancholy and sensitivity which really stand out as worthy of praise.

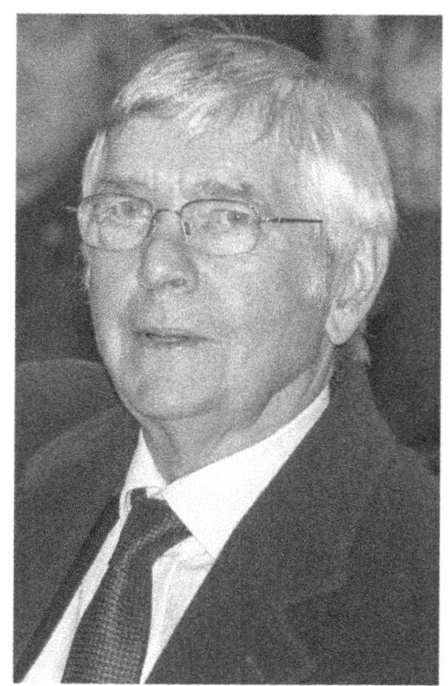

Sir Tom Courtenay

Although the play is essentially a two-hander, with Sally Carman providing a highly creditable expression of evocative yet subtle despondency as Stan's supportive but quietly sorrowful daughter, the small supporting cast is similarly solid. Eddie Capli makes the most of a dual role as a bus driver who visits Stan's lost property office – later revealed to be Ant, a member of the staff supporting Stan at the care home – while Kate Coogan brings restrained emotional power to her depiction of Dorrie, Stan's late wife. Dorrie's all-too-tangible presence in the world of her husband's fragmented memory emphasises his lasting sadness with regard to her passing, even in spite of the dementia that is affecting him, thus making her conspicuous absence in the present day seem all the more affecting.

Lost and Found is a drama which has a relatively short duration, but it is one which is imbued with understated intensity and delicate emotional significance. Worthy of praise is the production's highly unobtrusive sound design, which does a fine job of contrasting between the invitingly nostalgic milieu of Stan's professional past and the rather more clinical environment of his present, neatly separating his 'comfort zone' from the ambiguity of his current situation. Some reviewers noted at the time of the play's broadcast that as Stan's dementia is heavily suggested rather than explicitly interrogated, a number of interpretations are possible. Is his refuge in the past an involuntary response to his condition, underscoring a frustrating inability to orient himself in the present day? Or is it instead the manifestation of a desperate need to recall and revisit a bygone point in his life, when contentment and familiarity outweighed fear and uncertainty? Such is the shrewdly restrained skill of Kershaw's writing, both outcomes seem equally feasible depending upon the listener's own personal viewpoint.

By focusing on the vocal expressiveness of the cast, ably guided by Brown's robust direction, *Lost and Found* is at its most powerful when raising uncertainty over the definition of each character's individual identity. The gradual revelation of Stan's true circumstances, rooted in the modern day while clinging desperately to a bygone past, is effective precisely because the audience are forced to engage with the drama on its own terms – by focusing on dialogue and exposition, rather than the visual cues which have become more familiar through common exposure to cinematic or televisual presentation. We are encouraged to get to know Stan and his family, and even given the relative brevity of the play's running time there is ample opportunity to lay the foundation for a degree of emotional investment in the characters which makes the eventual payoff all the more effective – and harrowing. It is precisely because this everyman is so affable and agreeable that he becomes so relatable, bringing into sharp focus the fact that dementia, and the many issues which stem from it, could just as easily be affecting the listener or those close to them. Thus the shifting flexibility of personal characteristics which the protagonists must identify and overcome is a predicament which is uniquely dealt with by audio drama, and in a manner which is quite different from similar treatments of the subject in other nodes of popular media. In so doing, Kershaw and Brown succeed in creating a noteworthy production which – by dexterously interpolating themes of fractured identity onto a format which fully capitalises upon exploring both internal meditations and external communication of thoughts and actions to highlight the essentially indefinable nature of individual distinctiveness – brings a universal quality to the anxieties of ageing as well as the manifold difficulties that are posed by dementia.

19

THE QUIET POWER OF MONOLOGIC DISCOURSE

Maria Jastrzebska's Dementia Diaries

THE monologue has proven to be one of the most adaptable of literary devices, its roots extending back to at least the time of ancient Greece. Evident in many dramatic media, though most notably on the stage, the unique capacity of the monologue to allow characters a means of directly expressing their internal thoughts is one which would appear to pose a direct challenge to the depiction of dementia within a play or film. Much demand is placed upon a dramatist's skill to extrapolate how a character's inner voice can be explored with respect and accuracy when the physical and mental effects of dementia may make this conveyance uncertain or indistinct. Yet it was exactly this technical challenge which was to form the basis of *Dementia Diaries* (*Dziennik Demencji*), a 2009 stage drama by playwright Maria Jastrzebska.

Dementia Diaries is a play for five actors, accompanied by incidental music for flute and cello composed by Peter Copley. First performed as part of the LLL Anglo-Polish season in 2009, the production was supported by the East Sussex Arts Partnership and the Awards for All Big Lottery Fund. Featuring both British and Polish actors, the play takes place in a domestic setting where – in a series of overlapping monologues – different members of a family discuss their feelings about life and their current existence. Tata and Mama, a couple in late middle age, are affected by dementia. Their daughter (who is never named) and son Edzio consider the needs of their parents, eager to provide adequate support while simultaneously aware of the profound impact that a caring role has upon their own life. And domiciliary care worker Mrs Alicja, attentive to the family's dynamics while not actually a relation, provides an outsider's view of the familiar interactions as they unfold.

The characters do not interact with each other throughout the play, but instead address the audience directly – a strategy which Jastrzebska has described in interviews as being indicative of the way in which family members may sometimes hear each other without necessarily listening. Yet this approach is also strikingly effective in articulating the disjointed reality of dementia which is often explored in dramatic presentations, lurching from one viewpoint and frame of mind to another with little notice. Jastrzębska contests expectation in other ways, finding surreal humour in the way that the family comes to terms with the effects of dementia without ever making light of either them or the condition. This carefully calculated wit appears all the more dexterous for the relative sparseness of its inclusion; when the characters affected by dementia move unexpectedly from droll observations to moments of fear and forgetfulness, the juxtaposition makes the situation seem persuasively poignant.

The overlapping nature of the various monologues is highly effective, and not just in the way that the jarring quality of the technique encourages the audience to carefully consider the particular viewpoint of each character – as well as the numerous complicated ways in which they relate to one another. As press coverage from the time was to widely publicise, following its initial performances in 2009 the play was to be further developed with participation from health professionals based at Southampton's Memory Assessment and Research Centre (MARC) – a professional collaboration funded by the Wellcome Trust – which allowed the performers to meet with researchers and medical experts to further refine their characters' portrayals in terms of such crucially important areas as movement and the delivery of dialogue. This partnership ensured that the often-disordered communication of the characters who are affected by dementia is treated with accuracy as well as sensitivity, as is the very immediate nature of the difficulties (social, practical, and emotional) which bear down on the characters who are the providers of personal care.

One aspect of the play which especially impressed critics was the thoughtful manner in which Jastrzębska is able to express the effects of aphasia on the two characters with dementia. An inability to formulate or understand spoken language due to damage to particular regions of the brain, aphasia can be related to some forms of dementia, and here we see it manifested in occasional misunderstanding, characters struggling to find the right word, and in some cases choosing entirely the wrong expression to articulate something different from what they intended to communicate. Naturally this situation is highly frustrating for the characters who are affected by dementia, as well as their carers, and yet the dialogue manages to blunt the starkness of this exasperation by focusing instead on the occasional incongruity of the statements which are uttered and the illogicality of the resultant exchanges. Though these interactions sometimes evoke a humorous response from the audience, the intent is never to undermine the dignity of the characters; it is made clear in context that dementia is not being used as a means of ridicule, but rather that the laughter generated is simply a case of appreciating the humour caused by the farcicalities of ordinary life – something that anyone can relate to, whether their personal existence has been touched by dementia or not.

The skilled lyricism of Jastrzębska's dialogue is not surprising; an experienced poet, editor and translator, she has received a number of literary awards during her career (including the 2009 Off_Press International Writing Competition and the Fourth Troubadour International Competition in 2010). She has contributed to journals including the *Poetry Review* and *Los Angeles Review*, and her work has appeared in many anthologies over the years. Her numerous poetry collections, which have included *I'll Be Back Before You Know It* (2009) and *At the Library of Memories* (2013), have also been well-received. Jastrzebska uses *Dementia Diaries* in part to explore aspects of her own Polish cultural roots, having lived in the country as a child and retaining links to the nation in the years since, and her expression of dry East European wit does – at its best – echo that of the late, great Polish auteur Krzysztof Kieslowski in its restrained application. Accompanying the production, Copley's music – performed live on cello and flute – is similarly effective in that it mirrors both Jastrzebska's artistic intentions (honesty, frankness, even occasional tenderness) and stylistic application (subtlety and power in equal measure).

What is most laudable about the creative strategy of *Dementia Diaries* is Jastrzebska's unflinching desire to confront various issues simultaneously. While her depiction of dementia – and the stresses and difficulties which stem from the condition – has understandably received the greatest focus amongst commentators, she also unswervingly tackles other concerns facing the characters such as the social isolation and psychological impact which often accompanies a caring role, the difficulties in overcoming cultural disparities when living in a foreign land, and the perennial question of whether we truly ever communicate with each other in a manner which conveys our intent and needs with sufficient accuracy. This is further enhanced by the inspired contrast of attitudes between the characters; one of the parents has traumatic flashbacks to harrowing experiences during the Second World War, while the other is much more pragmatic even if her sense of the time she is living in seems somewhat vague. Their son, Edzio, translates much of his parents' situation in terms of risk assessment and medical safety, whereas his unnamed sister shifts from wonder to despondency and back again. And on the outside of the family but looking in with some bewilderment is Polish care worker Mrs Alicja, who seems as puzzled by the behaviour of Mama and Tata as she does by the fraught sensibilities of the couple's anxious offspring. Perhaps exactly because of the characters' extreme differences in mindset and approach to dementia, a wide-ranging picture is drawn of the family unit which emphasises both emotional needs and mutual support. Even when the spoken word fails, the audience is shown that love and family duty continue to provide the adhesive which keeps this disparate group of individuals bolstering each other and caring for one another's necessities even as the effects of dementia unrelentingly progress.

The play has continued to be performed over the years since Jastrzebska first composed it, including a national tour in 2011, and perhaps its lasting legacy has been the fact that – in its stark sincerity and often biting observation – it achieved a different kind of approach to dementia on stage in comparison to other monologic strategies which had previously been developed by by playwrights. Exhibiting a serrated commentary which reflects the lively creative essence of Alan Bennett without ever mimicking his distinctive performance style, and presenting as frank a portrayal of the effects of dementia as Tony Roper and Frank Differ's *Rikki and Me* (2006) (adapted from Kate Fulton's 2004 autobiographical text of the same name) – perhaps best remembered for Roper's touching soliloquy in the role of Glaswegian comedian Rikki Fulton as the veteran entertainer comes to terms with the enormity of a diagnosis of Alzheimer's Disease – *Dementia Diaries* has become an innovative benchmark for monologic explorations of the condition. With its quiet intensity and a clear willingness to balance the issues surrounding dementia with the understated absurdities of everyday life, Jastrzębska has produced a work which raises salient questions for anyone who has encountered dementia within their family unit, and which never tries to impose uncomplicated answers in an area where none exist to be found.

20

CONSTRUCTING AND EXPLORING A BOX OF MEMORIES

Brendan Murray's *Monday's Child*

THERE has rightly been much consideration in recent years of the difficulties and responsibilities facing young carers across the world. This topic has been explored in various artistic modes, particularly in recent years, and not only in terms of young people who are caring for people who are affected by dementia. Less common, however, have been examinations of the ways in which young people come to terms with the difficulties of the condition – and the effects that it has on those close to them – when deliberated specifically from the younger person's point of view.

Written by playwright Brendan Murray, the stage play *Monday's Child* was commissioned, produced, and toured by Tutti Frutti Productions in 2011-12, with a well-received run at York Theatre Royal in the spring of 2014. Initially directed by Wendy Harris, the artistic director of Tutti Frutti, it has since been produced by Barnstorm Theatre, Kilkenny under the direction of Philip Hardy, touring Ireland on three occasions between 2014 and 2016. Tutti Frutti has become especially well-known for its live theatre re-imaginings of fables and fairy tales, and *Monday's Child* was to use as its focus an exploration of dementia and memory as seen through the eyes of two central characters: an unnamed elderly lady, and her granddaughter.

Brendan Murray has led a long and distinguished career in professional theatre, producing plays for audiences ranging from youth to teens, families, and adults. Initially training as an actor at the Drama Studio London following a degree in drama in Huddersfield, he has since become well-known as a playwright and director. He has been Head of Theatre in Education at the Belgrade Theatre, Coventry (1982-85) and Writer in Residence at Sheffield's The Crucible Theatre (1989-90), and his work has been performed widely throughout the UK, Europe, Australia and North America. Murray has been the recipient of the Writer's Guild of Great Britain Award for Best Play: Children and Young People in 2009 and 2012, and was also to win the Brian Way Award in 2001. His teaching talents have been much in demand in universities and dramatic education institutions across the UK, and among his other professional posts he has been Visiting Gulbenkian Fellow at King's

College Hospital (2002-03) and Artistic Director of Oxfordshire (Touring) Theatre Company (2003-08).

The initial idea behind *Monday's Child* had been conceived by Wendy Harris, whose clear creative vision for the project ensured that it would meet a particular set of artistic goals: the play would be thought-provoking and yet light-hearted and good-natured, dialogue would be reasonably minimal, and there would not be too much of an emphasis on naturalistic realism. During the gradual evolution of the play, the development of the characters and situations would be achieved not solely through the dialogue provided by Murray, but also original music composed by Dominic Sales and Joanne Moven's choreography of the characters' movement. The result would ultimately be a somewhat impressionistic portrayal of the play's setting – the young girl's room, where her grandmother comes to visit – and the entire production has been lent a charming, otherworldly quality which is further accentuated by Catherine Chapman's inspired stage and costume design.

As the above summation may suggest, the events of *Monday's Child* are somewhat ambiguous and open to audience interpretation. An elderly woman (Erika Poole) comes to visit her granddaughter (Josie Cerise) one day, the young girl's living area appearing less like a room in a house and more as though it were some kind of surrealistic garden (thus emphasising the plethora of imaginative possibilities that it holds for young and old alike). Together, the pair dress up in outlandish clothing, perform song and dance routines, and explore the close bond that exists between them. As the play continues, they mutually begin to construct various recollections, their actions leading to consideration of what the concept of memory is and how it defines our experiences of life. However, the play is not just about constructing memories; it is also about the prospect of losing them. For the young girl, the encounter involves her gaining greater understanding of the challenges and occasional cruel truths about the world around her, but for her grandmother it is more about clinging to familiar certainties wherever possible while she slowly loses her grasp on reality as she previously understood it. In both cases, the overwhelming sense is one of revelling in the essential need to cherish every moment of our lives.

Monday's Child received research input from neuroscience specialists at Sussex University and the Alzheimer's Society, to ensure accuracy of its portrayal of memory loss, and yet Murray's script appears resolute in its determination to find ways of exploring the symptoms of dementia in a way that is life-affirming rather than melancholic. Principally designed for audiences of four to seven years old, the play's dialogue is never patronising in its attempts to relate complicated and often rather nebulous concepts in ways which young children will accept without difficulty. Grandmother and grandchild are referred to in the script merely as 'woman' and 'girl' respectively; it is up to the audience to decide what the nature of their relationship actually is, though the dialogue does heavily hint at the familial connection. The young girl sometimes becomes frustrated by the older woman's inability to remember things, but never to the point of annoyance or resentment; rather, her struggle to recall particular facts (such as what day of the week it is, for instance) throws light on the fact that for the girl, situating ourselves in a particular time and place is less important than rejoicing in the moment that we currently live in. It is a commendably constructive way of dealing with a potentially problematic issue.

Similarly, the beautifully-designed set lends a degree of ambiguity to the location of the pair's adventures. Is it the young girl's room, or perhaps an attic in the same house, filled with disparate boxes which contain abstruse and affecting memories? The branches of white trees nearby provide a useful means of draping props and costume items, but are they perhaps actually something more mundane such as coat-hangers in an adjacent closet, magically transformed by means of a youthful imagination? Just like the indefinable sense of time used by the play, the truth is that either interpretation seems equally valid; whatever the true location of their venue, the pair seem happy enough to use it as a launch-pad for their adventures as they dress up, dance, blow bubbles, experiment with the alphabet, and generally make the most of enjoying their time together.

Murray has wide-ranging experience of writing theatre for young people, and *Monday's Child* sees him at the very height of his powers in expressing the far-reaching ramifications of a challenging condition in ways which a youthful audience will find poignant, heart-warming and entertaining, but never worrisome or frightening. Throughout the play, the emphasis remains firmly on the importance of maintaining the bonds of friendship and family, mutual co-operation, and making the most of our life experiences – positive factors which people of all ages can extol and relate to. Because we see this intergenerational pairing as they make new memories, even if only the young girl has the capacity to retain them in the long term, the audience are encouraged to consider the value of memory and the way in which our recollections shape our image of ourselves and our lives. It is an elegant and commendably understated approach which brings alive concepts that otherwise may seem unclear and difficult to define.

With its affecting depiction of loss and gain, and playfulness and confusion, *Monday's Child* is an impressive theatrical experience which draws upon numerous strategies to achieve its artistic aims. The appealing central performances by Erika Poole and Josie Cerise (later succeeded by Noelle Brown and Iseult Casey for Irish productions of the play) help to ground the dreamlike staging in terms of reciprocated affection and collaboration, but they are aided every step of the way by Dom Sales's motivating compositions, the combination of grace and humour achieved by Joanne Moven's choreography of movement, and perhaps most especially Catherine Chapman's astonishingly inventive set design. Yet underpinning the entire production is Murray's moving and inspirational script, which so effectively pitches a young girl who loves to learn alongside an older woman whose predominant challenge is to retain some semblance of control over her increasingly unreliable memories. Thus for all its dexterity and evocation of childlike wonder and unfamiliar realities, the events of *Monday's Child* rest upon a simple but undeniably powerful premise that even when everything that defines us is compromised – whether memory, identity, or wellbeing – bonds of love and friendship can always endure.

21 GRACE, MOTION AND FREEDOM

The Chaturangan Dance Company and Fleeting Moments

FOR a condition which so regularly has a considerable impact upon movement and orientation, it is interesting to note the many ways that dementia has become the central topic of dance presentations in recent years. With its emphasis upon kinetic expression of freedom and refinement of movement, dance has significant potential to articulate complex emotion without words, bringing both immediacy and considerable intricacy to both choreographed and improvised narratives.

Among the most prominent of such dance performances has been *Fleeting Moments*, a high-profile artistic undertaking by the acclaimed Chaturangan Dance Company which combines a celebration of the value of people who are affected by dementia with an equally spirited defence of cultural diversity in the modern world. Under the experienced leadership of its artistic director, Bisakha Sarker MBE, the Chaturangan Dance Company has been popularising South Asian dance throughout the North-West of England and beyond for many years. A common theme running through the company's performances has been the vital need for greater cultural understanding throughout society in order to ensure tolerance, inclusion and community harmony. There is a very progressive twenty-first century ethos to this philosophy of mutual understanding, and yet it is one which has proven wide-ranging enough to present an artistic approach that is able to blend the traditional with the modern to very distinctive effect.

Fleeting Moments is among the most noteworthy artistic achievements in the history of the Chaturangan company to date; a dance performance which was specifically developed to be dementia-friendly from its very inception, the production featured live music and carefully developed audience participation following consultation with people living with dementia and their carers. First performed at The Bluecoat in Liverpool during February 2013, and developed through collaboration with the Arts Council and Liverpool City Council as well as Liverpool Hope University, *Fleeting Moments* brought to life a sensitive exploration of dementia through dance choreography as a means of celebrating cultural diversity in the modern world, thus emphasising the valued role that people with dementia have to play in society, irrespective of their age or cultural background.

Accompanied by varied musical styles throughout, the performance was divided into three distinct sections which drew upon technical characteristics of Indian dance, Chinese dance, and contemporary dance respectively. The emphasis was very much centred upon the life-enhancing qualities of dance as an art-form, and meaningful interaction with people who have dementia – as well as their carers and families – was at the very heart of the initiative. Audience participation was encouraged through a series of 'choreolabs', where director Sarker advanced spectator collaboration with the artists to devise new dance interpretations during the performance. These ranged from routines which were inspired by props such as an umbrella or polished stones, which signified 'beautiful moments' in the lives of participants, as well as using a work of poetry by Laurence Gardiner as the inspirational basis for a dance.

The diverse composition of the event's large audience was certainly in keeping with the Chaturangan organisation's aims of cultural multiplicity and mutual co-operation; with ages of the spectators ranging from youth through to people in the later years of life, representatives of many backgrounds were present including care professionals, students and academic researchers, writers and poets, third sector specialists, and many others. Everyone was encouraged to become involved in the performance at key points during the occasion. The result was a truly interactive experience which succeeded in the company's objective of encouraging greater awareness of dementia in addition to persuading individuals to directly involve themselves in interpretations of the condition through movement and physical expression. The event's approach heightened attentiveness towards the effects of the disorder while simultaneously accentuating the positivity of shared life experience irrespective of age, gender, sexual orientation, or cultural heritage.

One of the most admirable aspects of *Fleeting Moments* was the deliberate, multi-layered creative drive behind the performance. While the intention behind the choreographed dance sequences was to illuminate the unique potential of individual lives – emphasising that while dementia changes day-to-day living, it certainly should not devalue a person's significance in any way – the audience participation sections rejoice in the possibilities of the present, encouraging people to make the most of each waking moment. This overarching celebration of the human spirit provides a cohesiveness which underpins the Chaturangan Dance Company's multidisciplinary approach to *Fleeting Moments*; during the inaugural 2013 event, the dance sequences were complemented by additional expressive nodes such as visual arts provided by Noelle Williamson (sketches in pencil and watercolour inspired by the performances) and original music from Steve Boyland and Chris Davies. The overall effect was one of remarkable creative interconnection which emphasised the power of dance to enlighten, instruct, and inform.

As in the best dance routines, sometimes props which might otherwise seem innocuous are shown to have hidden consequence. The use of an umbrella, for instance, is on one level to employ an object which has widespread use, meaning that it is easily recognisable to someone whose sensory perception has been affected by dementia. It may bring back memories from a person's youth, or appear noteworthy in the present. Yet as Sarker explained during the event, it also functions as a kind of metaphorical shield; just as a physical umbrella is designed to shelter someone from rain, it might also be seen to have a symbolic representation as a defence which protects someone from the unpredictable 'weather conditions' that may be generated by the onset of dementia and its attendant symptoms. Again, the performance introduces an element of positivity which offsets the sense of isolation and apprehension surrounding dementia to instead offer new ways of dealing with the challenges of the condition.

The unerring professionalism of the Chaturangan Dance Company lies not just in the innovation and proficiency of their skilled dancers (which in the 2013 event included Anusha Subramanyam, Mary Pearson, Fenfen Huang, and Bisakha Sarker herself), but in the ways in which it realises the razor-sharp focus of its creative intentions. *Fleeting Moments* is deeply concerned with cutting through the constriction that is caused by seclusion and marginalisation, setting people free from unjust stigma so that they may realise a deeper level of self-esteem and personal confidence. At all times, the thrust of the performance is to empower people, helping them to realise their intrinsic value as an individual and exhorting society to embrace everyone, acknowledging that mental health is a challenge best met when people collectively work together to overcome wrongful attitudes. This is a powerful and positive message, and it is one which is so perfectly articulated by the intricate routines on display throughout the choreography and performance of *Fleeting Moments* that the presentation has continued to impress and inspire professionals and the public alike since the time of its debut.

In combining dynamic artistic expression with a contemplative focus upon specific needs ranging from the individual to the community at large, the Chaturangan Dance Company succeeded in using the vibrant multicultural backdrop of modern Britain to celebrate life in all of its manifold diversity. Under the leadership of artistic director Sarker, the organisation has continued to develop and refine *Fleeting Moments* as an ongoing project, delivering performances and workshops which have incorporated further opportunities for people who are affected by dementia to become involved in the expressive power of the medium of dance. With *Fleeting Moments*, the life-changing ramifications of dementia are never downplayed, nor are they in any way underestimated. Rather, the richly-layered choreography and the overriding inclusiveness of the performance's central philosophy enables the audience to overcome stereotypical responses to the condition, persuading them to look beyond preconception to address the feelings, the requirements, and the value of the individual.

22

ABSTRUSE EXISTENCE AND MALLEABLE REALITIES

Jackie Kay's Mind Away

IF there is one aspect of dementia which has endlessly fascinated writers, especially in the past few decades, it is the potential that the illness has to make us question the essential malleability of what we perceive as 'real'. There are few medical conditions which incline themselves more fully to Cartesian explorations of individual discernment of reality, forcing the reader out of their comfort zone as they are led to contemplate what it is that defines any one perception of existence as being somehow more 'authentic' than others.

Jackie Kay's one-act drama *Mind Away* was broadcast by Sky Arts in July 2009 as part of their ambitious *Theatre Live!* season, a run of six plays which included new work by leading writers as diverse as Kate Mosse and Michael Dobbs. The series was to enthuse critics at the time, who seemed to have developed an appetite for the kind of live broadcast drama which had previously been supplied by televisual conduits such as the stalwart *Play for Today* and its successors. The welcome return of original stage drama on the small screen was greeted with much excitement by many commentators, inevitably meaning that each play in turn was to receive close scrutiny, and this was especially true of *Mind Away* given that Kay was the writer who had accepted the daunting honour of penning the inaugural drama in the series. (The central story of the play was later to be adapted by Kay into prose form for her critically-acclaimed anthology *Reality, Reality* in 2012.)

Jackie Kay is a decorated and multiple award-winning Scottish writer whose work has spanned poetry, prose and drama. A graduate of the University of Stirling, she has been the recipient of the Saltire Society Scottish First Book Award, the Somerset Maugham Award, and the Guardian First Book Award Fiction Prize, amongst many others. Currently Professor of Creative Writing at Newcastle University, she was appointed Member of the Order of the British Empire (MBE) in 2006, and is also Cultural Fellow at Glasgow Caledonian University. She was elected a Fellow of the Royal Society of Edinburgh in 2016, and took up the position of Scots Makar that same year.

Over the course of a long and decorated career, Kay has dealt with many weighty issues in her prolific literary output. In choosing dementia as the central subject matter of *Mind Away*, she brings all of her distinctive contemplation and sensitivity of characterisation to the ways in which the condition can demonstrate far-reaching effects on family relationships as well as influencing an individual's ability to connect with an essentially allusive reality (given that, after all, never was a notion more given to shifting interpretation in a post-modern world). The result was an arresting performance experience which deftly blended existential issues with more immediate domestic concerns, ensuring that dementia was examined in an extensive and multiply-layered manner.

The play employs an elaborate dual narrative. The principal action concerns Nora (Sheila Reid), a sprightly woman in old age who is coping with the onset of dementia, who interacts with her feisty but warm-hearted daughter Mary (Siobhan Redmond), a novelist who has moved into Nora's flat following a painful break-up with her partner. During their playful interplay, where Mary does her best to buoy her mother through the painful difficulties of her condition by using her vivid creative imagination, the pair mutually decide that Nora isn't losing her memories – rather, they eventually determine, her recollections are being stolen by a handsome young doctor. They are unaware, however, that elsewhere in the city a certain Dr Mahmud (Raza Jaffrey) is finding his work constantly interrupted by a stream of consciousness that he cannot control – Nora's 'stolen' thoughts, manifesting themselves within Mahmud in unexpected and unwelcome ways, much to the consternation of his medical assistant (Lisa Livingston).

Mind Away presents its subject matter with real heart, greatly aided by earnest performances by Siobhan Redmond as a devoted but troubled daughter, and Sheila Reid's finely-controlled portrayal of Nora – an impressive depiction of a character who adroitly tilts from affectionate recollection to livid antagonism in an instant. It is much to the credit of Kay's skill as a writer, along with director Pip Broughton's keen eye for fine detail, that so many intricate layers of characterisation are hinted at dexterously without ever lingering on any one issue excessively. Mary is constantly fighting to keep Nora anchored in the immediate present, encouraging her mother to look forward with hope rather than continually harking back to bygone days that can be vaguely recalled and yet never truly re-lived. Yet Mary's own demons, reflected through her reliance on the bottle, are only too obvious to her mother in occasional, lucid moments of honest concern. Nora's perception of the present is sketchy and uncertain, leading her to revisit the past not out of yearning sentimentality, but rather so that she can secure herself within an authentic reality. Mary's struggle, then, is to present an optimistic future for her mother to reach for instead, even while she herself feels precious little sanguinity for her own expectations of life.

Regularly cutting across the main action, Raza Jaffrey gives a commendable performance as a troubled health care professional who finds himself facing his own uncomfortable questions about personal autonomy. His portrayal of quietly understated panic as he finds his own notions of reality under subtle assault (at one point he gives himself a Mini Mental State Examination to analyse the condition of his personal cognition), Mahmud is simultaneously unnerved and perplexed as Nora's life experiences continually intersect and overlap with his own. But is the doctor truly a discrete and autonomous individual, or simply a figment of Nora's increasingly fragmented imagination? Jaffrey's sincere and eminently restrained articulation of Mahmud's concerns leads to an unexpected and touching conclusion, which successfully communicates the play's overarching balance of thoughtfulness and tenderness.

Mind Away is a drama which combines congenial humour with bleak melancholy, and makes the most of its thirty-minute duration as it explores the extent to which an individual is a prisoner of their own perceptions. Considerable intricacy is packed into the play's comparatively brief running time, and yet as a viewing experience it feels neither rushed nor ever at risk of overstaying its welcome. By paralleling Mahmud's crisis of identity with Nora's deteriorating sense of self, Kay adroitly makes the point that dementia is a condition with a universal reach – no-one, not even the most skilled medical professional, can count themselves invulnerable from its onset. The tongue-in-cheek humour throughout the play never blunts the seriousness of the points that are made, nor the profundity of their significance. Is the juxtaposition of the real and the imagined one which is drolly amusing or heart-rending desolate? Only the individual has the power to discern where material authenticity ends and hyperreal self-awareness begins – a fact which is true not only of the play's characters, but of the audience too.

Key to *Mind Away* is the involvedness of the relationships which are depicted within the play's confines. Nora shows maternal empathy towards her daughter, and yet is seemingly frustrated by the listless direction of her child's life – a fact which is made glaringly obvious by occasional moments that exhibit anything but compassion. Mary struggles to embody the strong, reassuring figure that her mother so obviously needs to support her through the progression of her illness, yet is in the throes of internal torment due to the impact of relationship problems on her self-esteem and deep apprehension about the trajectory of her personal and professional future. Likewise, there is a sense of cunning dualism in the way that Mahmud's mounting uncertainty over his own atypical situation is balanced by the trepidation of his assistant, who is clearly concerned about her colleague's grip on reality. She is forced to watch, alarmed and seemingly powerless, as the talented doctor is reduced to a confused and fretful figure, fraught with doubt and hesitation over his perception of the here and now. It is a powerfully-realised dichotomy, and one which gives genuine pause for thought as the play advances towards its climax.

Jackie Kay's work has touched reflectively upon many weighty subjects including identity, family, and relationships, and with *Mind Away* she was to examine each of these subjects in unexpected but often highly meaningful ways. The play succeeds admirably in examining the complexities of dementia, conveying not only the alienation that the disorder can bring but also fleshing out the efforts required to combat its difficulties. The immediacy of live theatre, even via the medium of television broadcast, is especially well-suited to emphasising the unpredictability of behavioural shifts as well as (through some accomplished stage direction) challenging narrative expectations in powerful and genuinely unanticipated ways. Yet for all its narrative density and highly capable characterisation, it is the play's refusal to offer up any straightforward answers that remains longest in the mind; like the very condition that forms the focus of *Mind Away*, the storyline offers vagueness and ambiguities as it unfolds, but little in the way of concrete certainty. As with all perceptions of reality, the nature of authentic personal existence here seems fated to be recognisable only within the eye of the beholder.

23

JUBILATION AND APPREHENSION

The Sandglass Theater's D-Generation: An Exaltation of Larks

GIVEN its origins in ancient performance artistry, puppetry has proven to be an art form which has proven both versatile and surprisingly innovative. From the eighties political satire of ITV's infamous *Spitting Image* through to ventriloquist Nina Conti's success in more recent years with 'Granny', a witheringly acerbic elderly Scotswoman with a seemingly endless supply of sardonic put-downs, puppet acts have remained perennially popular with audiences – and often surprisingly subversive. Even cinema has presented some memorably alternative puppet-centric features over the years, including Peter Jackson's dark comedy *Meet the Feebles* (1989) and Brian Henson's detective parody *The Happytime Murders* (2018). But for all its proven effectiveness in formulating comedy through entertainment, what happens when puppetry is used to explore subjects of a more serious nature?

D-Generation: An Exaltation of Larks was the name of a daring but highly rewarding performance by Vermont's Sandglass Theater Company, a touring show which has been hosted at numerous venues including the famous Atlanta-based Center for Puppetry Arts in March 2015. A collaboration between experienced puppetry performers Eric Bass, Ines Zeller Bass and Kirk Murphy, the initiative sought to engage head-on with the demanding subjects of ageing and isolation. These are, of course, difficult topics for any form of art to deal with sensitively, so the choice of puppetry as a means of exploring them was a particularly bold one. In so doing, the artists behind the performance proved the adaptability and depth of narrative that is possible through the use of puppets in communicating complex themes for mainstream audiences.

Sandglass Theater was established in 1982, and quickly became established as a leading ensemble company which has performed in dozens of countries across the world. Though their performers have appeared in many international venues, they also host presentations at their own theatre in Putney, Vermont, where instructional teaching in puppetry also takes place. The organisation has been the recipient of numerous prizes for their work.

D-Generation: An Exaltation of Larks traces its thematic origins to a number of visits made by the Company's arts practitioners to a group of elderly people living in the Pine Heights at Brattleboro Center for Nursing and Rehabilitation, a care facility based in Vermont. The individuals with whom they interacted had each received a diagnosis of dementia, and during their communication with residents the performers took great care to note their reactions and views on a number of personal issues – a process which was aided by 'Timeslips', a pioneering model of creative storytelling which was developed by researcher Anne Basting. The overarching purpose behind this approach was to build up a picture of the concerns facing people with dementia in modern life, along with the effects that their condition has upon their families and carers at all points in its progression. Through this method, they uncovered a collage of penetrating emotions which ranged from nostalgia to fear, where warm recollection existed alongside apprehensive disorientation. Thus when the time came to translate these experiences into a stage performance, the full spectrum of life was there for all to see: the indomitability of the human spirit is celebrated, while the harmful and upsetting effects of the condition are simultaneously laid bare.

With *D-Generation*, the Sandglass Theater Company proved why their approach has won so many admirers amongst audiences and the critical community alike. Using diminutive but often disconcertingly life-like puppets of elderly individuals, operated by rods rather than strings, the performance relies upon a non-linear narrative which eschews any imposition of a conventional three-act structure. Artists Bass, Murphy and Zeller

Bass bring these characters to life in a manner which emphasises individual personalities, accentuating the fact that a diagnosis of dementia requires commitment from family members, carers and health care professionals alike to ensure that the personal distinctiveness of those affected by the condition is respected at all times.

As the title of the performance suggests, there is considerable celebration of the individual to be found here, and the importance and value of life can be witnessed in abundance. Yet for all the artists' skilful lightness of touch, the play does not shirk from the weighty consequences which so often accompany the symptoms of dementia. Confrontation of social stigma, the loneliness of isolation, and the distress of difficult and often incoherent recollection are all brought into sharp focus as the performance progresses. Sparing use of pre-recorded video footage recorded by Michel Moyse and a haunting, wistful musical score by Paul Dedell combine with the central puppetry to striking effect, creating an on-stage environment that has the ability to be both vibrantly expressive and occasionally disquieting.

With the three performers taking on the personae of care home employees, constantly interacting with the various puppet characters who are portraying the facility's residents, the play is estimable in its determination to advance respect and consideration at all times towards people who are affected by dementia. The feelings and recollections which are related to the audience, which had been shaped by the performers' many research visits to care home residents during the play's development, seem all the more immediate for the deliberate contrast between subtle, humorous observations and moments of intense, private trepidation. Because of the non-linear mode of storytelling which results, the experiences which are conveyed are lent both pathos and sincerity that bring a touching level of authenticity to proceedings.

Various critical accounts of the production highlighted the determination of Sandglass to actively promote the significant level of creative potential that still exists within someone who is affected by even late-stage dementia; where lucid expressions and conventional narratives may become impossible, sounds and images may still hold a key to articulating moods and emotions. The end result of this philosophy does not always make for easy or straightforward watching, but it nonetheless creates a dramatic presentation which is stimulating, sincere in its artistic principles, and often compellingly poetic.

The puppets employed in *D-Generation* were designed by Coni Richards, Jana Zeller and Ines Zeller Bass, and brilliantly communicate through body language and facial expressiveness the complex mixture of feelings that are imparted throughout the performance. While puppetry in popular theatre received a significant boost at the turn of the century as a result of Robert Lopez and Jeff Marx's well-received and highly successful Broadway musical *Avenue Q* (2002), the subject matter behind puppet performance has varied dramatically as the field has assertively attempted to shake off persistent supposition that it is a discipline which is predominantly geared towards light entertainment and youth audiences.

Sandglass neatly cuts through these misconceptions by presenting a mature, thought-provoking theatrical experience which genuinely confronts assumptions about dementia and the experience of growing older. The Company received funding to produce *D-Generation* from a variety of sources, including The Clowes Fund, Fresh Sound Foundation, the National Endowment for the Arts, and the world-famous The Jim Henson Foundation, and it comes as no surprise that this enervating theatrical piece has been staged many times since its first appearance before audiences. While some reviewers may not have considered puppetry to be a likely medium for defying audience expectation when it came to themes that derive from dementia, in truth the cast – both human and puppet alike – do an exceptional job of using this subversion of anticipation to truly encourage open minds and new ways of thinking about the condition.

With its effortless transition from light-hearted playfulness to thoughtful melancholy – and then back again – *D-Generation: An Exaltation of Larks* is a production which fully explores the ability of puppetry to command complex emotion and nuanced sentiment, bringing to life not only fully-realised characters but also a wide range of uncomfortable issues – nervousness, loss, seclusion, and discomfiture are all addressed at various points throughout the show. For any drama to address these topics so directly would be admirable evidence of artistic integrity, but in employing puppets in the place of conventional lead actors the performers are also able to play dexterously with audience expectancy in highly effective ways, encouraging the viewer to challenge their own anticipated responses to the action that is playing out on the stage before them. In so doing, the Sandglass Theater Company proved themselves to be at the forefront of advancing new techniques to truly make the most of a well-established performance genre, while simultaneously conveying a multifaceted and adeptly layered narrative approach to a subject whose very nature demands sensitivity and respect.

24
BRIDGING LAUGHTER AND DESPONDENCY
Patrick Jones's Before I Leave

WHILE in recent years there have been an increasing number of dramas which have examined the impact of dementia upon individual lives and the everyday existence of people who care for those affected by the disorder, less widespread have been plays which instead focus upon the impact of dementia upon communities. Yet with a greater focus upon strategies at local, regional, and national level towards providing dementia-friendly communities which aim to ensure that accessibility is maximised to support people who have the condition, it seems only fitting that this vitally important issue should be explored in greater detail through the arts. While it is a matter of crucial significance to ensure that people with dementia are ensured safe, supported access to amenities such as public transport, retail outlets, and municipal facilities, just as important is the need to foster an understanding attitude amongst the community at large. Such an approach ensures not only that people who have dementia are safeguarded in their daily business to the best possible standard, but also that the fundamental role played by the community in supporting vulnerable people is equitably highlighted.

Before I Leave is a musical stage drama written by prolific poet and playwright Patrick Jones. Inspired by the true-life story of Merthyr Tydfil's Cwm Taf Choir, a choral group established in support of people who have been diagnosed with dementia and supported by the Alzheimer's Society, the play relates the experiences of six separate people whose lives are connected with the common theme of dealing with the condition in one way or another. Set against a polarised political backdrop, *Before I Leave* deals with several hard-hitting social issues – not least the devastating effects of sweeping cuts to public services in communities across Britain. Yet for all its ideological concerns, it is not primarily a play about political philosophies and principles; rather, its concerns centre upon the extensive effects of government policies on the lives of ordinary people, and how individuals must act collectively if they are to endure in times of difficulty.

Born in Monmouthshire and especially well-known as a literary figure in his native Wales, Patrick Jones is a writer with a long professional history of supporting the study of literature in communities. Having taught adult literacy at Blackwood Community College and the Ebbw Vale Institute, he established the Blackwood Young Writers Group – based at the Blackwood Miners Institute – in 1993, and has gone on to launch further reading and writing workshops at many schools and youth centres. He was a creative literacy worker for the Cynon Project, and was appointed writer in residence at Swansea College in 1988. Jones is a politically active writer, and has publicly supported numerous charitable organisations as well as being involved as a high-profile figure in several protests. His poetry and drama has engaged with a wide range of pressing, socially-conscious issues, and often emphasises the pressures placed on traditional communities by changing socio-cultural priorities and government decisions at the national level.

Before I Leave debuted in 2016, produced by The National Theatre Wales as part of the Festival of Voice Cardiff. The play was inspired by Jones's experiences of community-based choirs which supported people with dementia; encountering the phenomenon shortly after his own uncle had died from vascular dementia, Jones was impressed by the camaraderie and mutual support that was on display, as well as the incredible power of music to reach people even when they had become profoundly affected by the condition. Fascinated by the concept of 'musical memory' and the ability of music to stimulate deep emotional responses, he visited a number of different choirs around Wales (each of them supported by the

Alzheimer's Society) as part of a community project, and took note of the positive ways that the members engaged with and responded to the songs that were being performed.

However, while captivated by the meaningful ways that the choirs he witnessed had improved the lives of those who participated in them, Jones did not evade the harmful combination of issues that were affecting local communities. The characters who appear throughout the play are by no means idealised, and the area in which they live is under pressure as never before. It is this amalgamation of domestic stresses and socio-cultural tensions that lends such relevance and human relatability to *Before I Leave*, and which makes it such a memorable theatrical experience.

Its inaugural performance directed by Matthew Dunster, *Before I Leave* is based around the experiences of a Welsh community choir which supports people who are affected by dementia in a one-time mining area. Meeting at the town's local library, the members include Rocky (Dafydd Hywel), a former coal miner, and Evan (Desmond Barrit), a retired policeman, who had once clashed across the picket lines during the miners' strike of the 1980s but who now – both in their eighties – collaborate side by side in the choir, their memories of the past clouded by the progression of their shared condition. Joe (Martin Marquez), in his fifties, is affected by the early onset of Alzheimer's Disease; an avowed music devotee, he attends the choir with his wife Dyanne (Melanie Walters). The pair had first bonded over their shared love of music, but Joe is struggling with the enormity of his diagnosis and finds himself deeply troubled by the impact of the condition, leading to behavioural turbulence and violent mood swings. The choir also includes former librarian and opera aficionado Marge (Gaynor Morgan Rees), whose commanding vocal talents are being ravaged as the result of dementia on her body, and the somewhat hard-hearted Siobhan (Sara McGaughey), whose mother is resident in a care home due to the condition. Siobhan refuses to visit her parent, reasoning that as her mother is unable to recognise or respond to conversation, she sees little point in taking the time to call on her. (Others are aghast at her lack of empathy, with Dyanne asserting that the older woman will be aware of Siobhan's absence and will likely welcome the company, even if she now lacks the ability to react and reply.)

The choir members perform various cover versions throughout the play, drawing on the music of Tom Jones, The Jam, Queen, The Sex Pistols, Elvis Presley, David Bowie, and even Lady Gaga. *Before I Leave* also features as its title song an original composition by Nicky Wire and James Dean Bradfield of the Manic Street Preachers (Wire being the brother of playwright Jones). In the grand tradition of other triumph-over-adversity tales in crumbling, underfunded community settings – such as films including Mark Herman's *Brassed Off* (1996) and Stephen Daldry's *Billy Elliot* (2000) – the choir finds itself facing a premature end due to the closure of the local library as a result of funding cuts, much to the dismay of the their leader Scott (Oliver Wood).

What follows is an attempt to save the choir, eventually culminating in the group auditioning for the ITV show *Britain's Got Talent*.

With so much attention-grabbing music on offer, it would be all too easy for the audience to concentrate solely on the play's emphasis upon the potential for music to bring people and communities together, but in truth that would be to tell only part of the story. For if *Before I Leave* focuses on the proud heritage of Wales in the form of its choral tradition, it also highlights the country's history of protests in support of social justice. There is almost a sense of Spenglerian cyclical history in the way that the miners' strike and 1980s public service cuts are mirrored in the era of the so-called 'Big Society', where mental health care is under increasing pressure and social services are being stretched to breaking point. Thus while the play contains ample good humour, there is genuine concern on display regarding the inability of society to effectively combat social isolation, or the level of empathy and individual respect that is on offer in many care homes. Similarly, the life-affirming exploration of the choir's ability to give its members a positive outlet for their creative impulses does nothing to blunt the personal difficulties that unfold for its various adherents; we witness Evan's exploitation at the hands of his avaricious daughter, and are forced to consider the uncomfortable situation facing Joe, whose occasionally aggressive reactions raise unnerving questions about the detrimental effects of dementia on his personality.

Before I Leave is a complex and uncompromising play which blends its depiction of dementia on individual lives with wider issues surrounding the pressures on local communities, and to admirable effect. While there is no mistaking Jones's clarion call to communities around the country, urging them to harness people power in order to better meet the challenges of a changing world, similarly no-one can deny his similarly sincere plea to break through the stigma surrounding mental health and better understand the difficulties which are posed by dementia. At various points, the play underscores with great confidence the fact that while the condition presents enormous difficulties to an individual's mental and physical health, it also has the potential to cause various other issues – to families, friends, communities, and society at large. While Jones never simplistically posits the notion that greater social comprehension of the condition can somehow eradicate these difficulties altogether, he does make the point that if each of us takes the time to show greater compassion towards people who are affected by mental health problems – and react not with uncertainty, but empathy towards our fellow citizen – there can be great improvement in public consideration towards conditions such as dementia, improving the lives of many as a result.

Video Games and Interactive Entertainment

25

A JOURNEY TO MANIA AND DEMENTIA

Bethesda Softworks's The Elder Scrolls: The Shivering Isles

WHILE dementia is a condition which has posed numerous challenges for directors and musicians when it comes to depicting the disorder in an accurate, respectful, and truthful manner, it is important to note that over the years its portrayal has been a matter of similar import for creators of interactive entertainment. Whether on personal computers, video game consoles or mobile devices, there has been a vast increase in the numbers of people across the world who regularly engage with interactive scenarios, and regardless of platform these gaming experiences have diversified dramatically over the years to embrace just about every possible kind of narrative. With programmers keen to demonstrate their storytelling capabilities as much as their prowess at stretching the resources of computer systems, it is no surprise that dementia – and other forms of mental illness – have featured within interactive experiences over the decades that home computers have been a part of modern life. However, given the multifarious nature of the disorder, it has proven to be a perennial challenge for game designers when it comes to representing its symptoms in a precise and suitably authentic manner, meaning that depictions of the condition have varied widely in terms of their presentation.

The *Elder Scrolls* games have firmly cemented a reputation amongst the console and computing community as being amongst the most sophisticated fantasy role-playing games ever devised, with successive entries in the series winning their creators Bethesda Softworks an array of high-profile awards – numerous coveted Game of the Year plaudits among them – for their detailed environments, complex quests, and open-ended scenarios. At time of writing, the series has sold more than 50 million units across all entries in the *Elder Scrolls* cycle, with particular success being noted for major instalments such as *Morrowind* (2002), *Oblivion* (2006), and *Skyrim* (2011). But amongst the detailed histories and rich characterisation of the *Elder Scrolls* games lies an oft-unexplored angle of the series; namely its complex and ingenious engagement with the subject of mental health disorders.

In *The Shivering Isles*, a 2007 expansion to *Oblivion* – the bestselling fourth game in the series – Bethesda were to present an environment which was altogether quite different from the acclaimed swords-and-sorcery milieu which had become synonymous with the *Elder Scrolls* series. Suddenly supplanting the familiar fantasy kingdom of Tamriel (where the majority of the series' action has taken place) was a much more surreal and at times sinister place: an alternative dimension known as the Shivering Isles. Ruled over by a powerful demon, the self-styled Daedric Prince of Madness known as Sheogorath (a sort of otherworldly supporting character since the series' earliest days), the isles formed an ethereal realm which was split into two opposing blocs: Mania and Dementia. Use of the term 'madness' in relation to mental stability does, of course, inevitably risk seeming unenlightened and dangerously ill-considered to many, even within a fantasy context. But however dramatic the terminology may have appeared, there was no doubting the strikingly unique nature of the two distinct environments which were being presented to the player.

Just as these two dominions stand apart from the mundanities of the real world, so too do they prove to be starkly dissimilar from each other. Mania is brightly-coloured and exuberantly designed, whereas dementia is dark, dreary and foreboding. While the former region is characterised by its colourful grassland areas and giant fungus-like trees, the latter is a grim marshland filled with fetid swamps and petrified trees. The juxtaposition could not be more visually marked, and it also extends to the lands' inhabitants: the denizens of Mania are high-spirited and prone to overexcitement, while those living in Dementia are depressive and miserable. Key to both is an underlying air of subtle tyranny: order is maintained in Mania by the disconcerting Golden Saints, a kind of wraithlike militia force; their counterparts in Dementia are the sinister Dark Seducers.

It quickly becomes apparent that the binary opposition of these contrasting communities – divergent and yet complementing each other – has much in common with their unpredictable master. In spite of seemingly conducting a perpetual war against Jyggalyg, the Daedric Lord of Order, Sheogorath seems oblivious to a particularly harsh reality: he is, in fact, eventually revealed to be the very same person that he is fighting against. Thus the two disparate parts of the Shivering Isles form a kind of living representation of Sheogorath's inner conflict; Mania epitomises the strange ebullience of his unrestrained psychoses, whereas Dementia is the embodiment of the darker, more despondent aspects of his character. The player discovers that the entire realm is, in a very real sense, locked into a constant struggle not only with itself but also with its polar opposite – a living allegory of Sheogorath's crisis of personality.

So can a visit to the Dementia of the Shivering Isles lend anything to our real-life understanding of the condition? Certainly it cannot be denied that Bethesda's portrayal of Dementia's terrain is stylistically striking; tangled roots spring out from the landscape, deterring even the most ardent of adventurers and leading unwary travellers to become hopelessly lost. The weary oppressiveness of the area's permanently overcast gloom and the paranoid, discouraging interactions of its inhabitants combine to depict an environment which is as dreamlike as it is disorienting. But the ultimate sense is that the player is witnessing a realm which has been constructed by external notions of how the symptoms of dementia may be conceived and reconstructed within an explicitly unreal setting, rather than deliberately attempting to provide a first-person evocation of any aspect of the condition itself.

It could be claimed, of course, that there is a larger moral question at hand here: namely whether dementia, or any other mental disorder, can ever provide suitable raw material for the backdrop of a fictional narrative in a meaningful, ethical manner. Bethesda certainly makes a commendable attempt at proving that, if achieved sensitively, this goal can indeed be attained within a fantasy context. The land of Dementia neither trivialises nor sensationalises the condition for which it is named, but certainly does an admirable job of depicting different facets of the disorder via indirect and, at times, almost coded means. This is not a game which employs dementia as a glib shorthand for mental turmoil or emotional confusion, but rather as a genuine starting point for a much more consequential exploration of an inventive mind which has been drawn into all-out war with itself.

Because the main character is able to step out of the highly-structured, open-ended quest narrative of the main *Oblivion* game to explore this alternate dimensional reality, there is no immediate time pressure to complete the *Shivering Isles* expansion within a set duration, leaving the player free to explore at their leisure (and return to the main game's Province of Cyrodiil, and the principal quest, at any point of their choosing). By becoming Sheogorath's protégé, the protagonist is charged with ensuring that the isles survive destruction, and while the expansion contains opportunities to hone skills and increase experience points in much the same manner as the main game, its true strength shines through in the vastly dissimilar world that it creates. Gone is the verisimilitude of the main quest, with its exactingly-detailed villages and feudalistic towns, in favour of a bizarre landscape where just about anything can happen. As in the central game, quests can be completed in succession, or the player can go off the beaten track and attempt various sidequests on their journey. This allows for a suitably immersive playing experience which emphasises the sheer sense of contrast between the isles' opposing realms, giving gamers the opportunity to investigate the region's denizens as well as its many dangers. It is precisely because of the way in which players are encouraged to explore these various areas and settlements that the conclusion to the expansion scenario feels so much more satisfying: after eventually defeating Jyggalyg, it is revealed that the Prince of Order had been cursed by his fellow demons to constantly alternate between his true persona and that of Sheogorath, thus being doomed to an unremitting cycle of destruction and reincarnation. By unwittingly breaking this sequence of events, the player is now named as the successor to Sheogorath – the new Prince of Madness – and as such becomes the embodiment of the Shivering Isles in all their struggles and oppositions.

The conflicts and internal discord articulated throughout the game are thoughtfully employed; certainly there is allegorical resonance in Jyggalyg's inability to hold the symptoms of his condition at bay, thus transforming him into a different individual entirely. Events build towards a conclusion which presents a kind of unforgiving logic that defies the carefully-engineered absurdity of the outlandish environment in which it is situated. One may well expect such refined game dynamics from a series which has sold copies in the tens of millions, but such a carefully-measured interpretation of the limits (and potential) of individual perception may perhaps be less anticipated. While not played quite as widely as the main *Oblivion* game, *The Shivering Isles* was nevertheless praised by reviewers for attempting something genuinely new within the confines of the venerable *Elder Scrolls* franchise. While the game's exploration of dementia and mania as explicit 'shades of madness' may naturally divide the sensibilities of many, due to its direct projection of complex mental health symptoms onto the dynamics of an entire environment, *The Shivering Isles* does unquestionably present a courageously detailed depiction of an often disconcerting battle between order and chaos. Because it is made clear from the beginning that the reality experienced throughout Mania and Dementia may well be only the closest approximation of corporeal materiality that the human mind can comprehend, players are ultimately guided to question how we perceive our own existence, and to ask what the implications are for authenticity of experience in a realm where everything seems to be in flux and nothing can truly be proven to be either tangible or true.

26

DEMENTIA IN THE DIGITAL DOMAIN

CRL Software and Mel Croucher's iD

THERE has been some discussion in recent years amongst academics and researchers with regard to the way in which dementia (and mental health conditions in general) has been conveyed in video games of various different genres. From first-person shooters to mystery games, the condition is being explored in far-reaching and often inventive ways as never before, thanks to a games industry that has increasingly embraced both artistic creativity and the issues posed by real-life difficulties in equal measure. Due to the graphical sophistication and processing power of the latest gaming technology, detailed and sometimes disturbing depictions of dementia have been brought into the public eye over the past decade in particular, and in ways which have challenged assumptions about the ability of video games to examine the disorder in a thought-provoking and sensitive manner. However, a willingness to engage with mental health issues is actually far from a new development in computer games, and its origins can be traced as far back as the mid-1980s.

In Margaret Thatcher's Britain, the home computer revolution was a major triumph for UK industry, and at the forefront of the movement was Cambridge's famous Sinclair Research Ltd. Founded by Clive Sinclair, later knighted for his services to British industry, the Sinclair ZX Spectrum home computer would become the first introduction for many people to digital computing technology outside of the workplace. In its heyday, the machine would sell some five million units across its various models released throughout the 1980s. By today's standards, the ZX Spectrum seems a hopelessly primitive machine, loading its programs from a standard cassette tape and possessed of a limited bank of memory (the most popular model boasted 48Kb of total RAM; smaller than a modest present-day e-mail message). Yet the humble Sinclair Spectrum was home to some of the most innovative games of the time, and would play host to what can arguably be considered the world's earliest computer simulation of dementia symptoms.

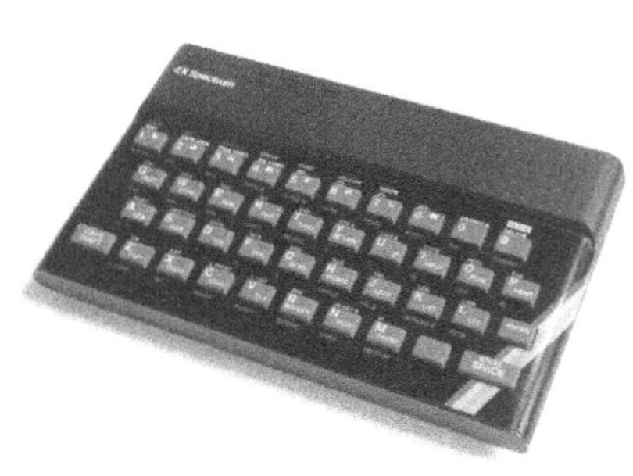

The Sinclair ZX Spectrum

Providing a convincing psychological replication of a condition as complex as dementia would be a daunting prospect for even today's advanced computing technology; back in the eighties, the very concept seemed unthinkable. But pioneering programmer Mel Croucher was never a man to let expectation curtail his ambitions. Though his name is rarely heard today outside of the retro-gaming world, Croucher was a legend of the British 8-bit computing scene – a groundbreaking free thinker who effortlessly redefined generic conventions even in an industry noted for its creative flexibility. He founded Automata UK – considered one of the UK's earliest software houses – in 1977, just prior to the home computer boom of the eighties. Developing wildly eccentric games which inspired many later programmers, including the award-winning *PiMania* (1982) and early multimedia title *Deus Ex Machina* (1984), Croucher's titles defied categorisation just as their sheer inventiveness left many consumers scratching their heads in bafflement. However, by making many of his games available over radio broadcast – meaning that they could be recorded to cassette and then loaded onto the Spectrum – he ensured that his quirky style would soon reach a wide and dedicated audience.

A games designer who was well ahead of his time, in 1986 Croucher was to create a title which many would herald as being amongst the most elaborate of all his projects: *iD*. Collaborating with Colin Jones, a similarly ambitious and unconventional programmer who was perhaps best-known at the time for his interactive fiction, *iD* was the type of game that disregarded anything even approaching an easy explanation. A wholly text-based experience, stylistically similar – at face value – to many of the adventure games which were hugely popular at the time, *iD* soon proved to be no ordinary computing experience. The title was published by the prominent CRL publishing house (under their Nu-Wave label), whose charismatic owner, Clement Chambers, was keen to showcase a gaming experience that featured artificial intelligence – an area of great interest in the 1980s. *iD* came with little in the way of user instructions, leaving the player largely on their own from the minute they load up the program. Immediately they are presented with a one-to-one interaction between themselves and a digital entity, which prompts them to ask – and respond to – various questions. Is the purpose of the game to ascertain the identity of the artificial intelligence who is replying to the user's queries? Or rather, is the player assisting that intelligence to determine their own personal identity? Only one thing seemed to be certain: that no two people were ever to have the same experience when engaging with the game.

So how does *iD* present a gaming environment that connects us to, or explores, issues relating to dementia? Certainly the program's title alludes to a number of different aspects of its function. Firstly, it refers most obviously to unique individual identity (or ID). Then it is suggestive of the id, from Freud's structural model of psychic apparatus. And finally, there is an allusion to computer science, where an identifier (ID) uniquely identifies a specific record or object. All three of these aspects come to play a part in the way that the game interprets the nature of individual psychology and explores what it means to be an autonomous individual. Crucially, the artificial intelligence in the game seems unsure of its character, its personality, and even its own unique characteristics. It requires user input to help it string together fragmentary memories and past experiences in order to ascertain its basic nature. This builds trust (which is measured by an on-screen meter), thus opening it up to further questioning. Should the player demonstrate inconsistency, perhaps inclining the in-game character to feel that it is being lied to, then trust will falter. Croucher's love of wordplay was more than evident throughout, and the questions fired at the player will often give them pause for thought as they deliberate on the most effective response. The intelligence is also prone to variations in mood, announcing that it feels – for instance – elated or depressed at any given time. The way that it responds to the user's questions is predicated upon the state of its mood, as well as its interpretation of the tone and content of the player's line of enquiry.

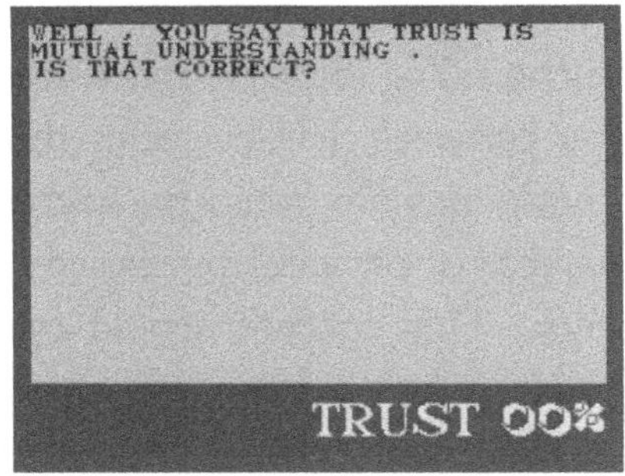

iD

iD does not explicitly refer to dementia, but – such is its enigmatic approach to its subject matter – it perhaps does not have to. This is a game which puts at its centre the experience of conscious thought. Confusion surrounding identity, and a need to recognise distinguishing personal characteristics though interaction with the contiguous environment, encourages consideration of all aspects of personal psychology and individual independence. This concept would seem commendable enough today, when postmodern aspects of artificial intelligence development seem ever more relevant, but this was a game developed in the mid-eighties which took up less memory than would be required to display a website logo on a modern PC. While the limitations of the technology clearly mean that *iD*'s artificial intelligence is in no danger of passing the much-discussed Turing Test, as a model for depicting complex psychology on a rather unassuming technological platform the game would influence many later coders and certainly laid the early groundwork for considerably more sophisticated depictions of dementia that we have come to recognise in modern video gaming.

Mel Croucher remains active in computer games programming today, as a journalist, software developer and sometime broadcaster. In 2012, he reformed Automata UK in the form of Automata Source Ltd., and has also been appointed head of the Jeeni streaming data service. An author who is as comfortable with writing technical textbooks as he is with comedy fiction, he has spoken in recent interviews of his excitement that the independent spirit of homebrew app development for today's mobile devices has reignited something of the creative passion that characterised the early days of computing and helped to make that period so memorable. Amongst his many pursuits has been the resurrection of some of his earlier work, reinterpreting these experimental programs for modern technological platforms, and thus it remains to be seen whether *iD* will be revisited in the years ahead. Certainly it would be an intriguing prospect to witness Croucher's ground-breaking program let loose on today's PCs, and to see what kind of form a modern remake may ultimately take. But whatever may happen in the future, there is no doubting the game's significance in its original eighties format, or the sweeping aspiration which helped to make the title stand out from the crowd in a market that was saturated by literally thousands of competitors.

27 EXPLORING DARK CORNERS OF THE MIND

AGaming+'s Dementia

DEMENTIA is a condition which has only sparingly been addressed throughout the history of computer gaming, at least until recently, and it is even more uncommon to witness it being presented as the central theme of a title rather than an incidental aspect of it. However, in a distinctive mobile gaming experience by independent Ukrainian software developers AGaming+, the effects of dementia have been given centre stage in a manner which has proven to be both arresting and genuinely thought-provoking.

AGaming+ have released numerous gaming apps over the years, several of them dealing with mental health in some capacity or another – albeit usually in the context of thriller-style games, most especially the first-person perspective survival horror *Mental Hospital* series (2013-), the entries in which have generally taken a more melodramatic approach to psychiatric illness. Several of the company's other games have, however, been more thoughtful in their modus operandi, including suspenseful adventures *Dead Bunker* (2013), *The Light* (2013), and *The Sun: Origin* (2017). While a majority of their titles have their foundations in the horror genre, many also exhibit a keen understanding of the psychological – not least their dark, claustrophobic mind-control thriller *A-2184* (2014). They have honed their talent for generic cross-pollination to good effect, producing games which riff on supernatural horror, forebodingly oppressive environments, and genuinely surprising plot twists.

Released in December 2013 as a download from the Google Play Store for Android mobile devices, the game – simply entitled *Dementia* – was available free to those wishing to try out the opening stage ('First Day'), but an additional payment was required to play the three subsequent chapters ('Night of Fear', 'Second Day' and 'Night of Truth'). The game puts the player in the role of an unnamed protagonist who finds themselves alone in an abandoned house. The game's instructions are sparing, suggesting that the protagonist is possessed of a kind of supernatural 'sixth sense' and that they have been summoned to an abandoned mansion to investigate the mysterious disappearance of previous occupants. Local people in the area have apparently termed this missing persons phenomenon 'the dementia', and over the course of their investigations the player will gradually discover why this is the case.

Like many other point-and-click first person mystery games of this nature – not least Cyan Worlds' pioneering *Myst* (1993), which kick-started the genre and spawned a multitude of imitations – very few explicit plot details are made known to the player ahead of time for the purposes of setting the scene. Beyond the game's scant guidance notes, participants are more or less thrown in at the deep end, and part of the game's objective is to establish (even in abstract terms) what is actually going on within the eerie confines of the abandoned mansion house before ways of engaging with the narrative strategy are fully determined.

At least initially, *Dementia* hints at an ostensibly supernatural plotline, complete with an eerie sense of foreboding and occasional (somewhat pervasive) occult imagery. However, it takes little time for the player to realise that the 'haunted house' conceit is actually masking a rather more profound objective on the part of the creators. Peering beyond the shadows and the echo of footsteps along deserted corridors, it soon becomes clear that the derelict mansion has been consciously intended to function as an allegory for dementia itself. Specific visual and auditory effects are carefully employed in a deliberate attempt to highlight some of the symptoms of dementia in a realistic and considerate way. This is achieved by various means, from the disorientation caused by the protagonist's 'second sight' through to hallucinatory phenomena which becomes apparent in various areas of the mansion's interior environment. Because the building is deliberately capacious and given to the

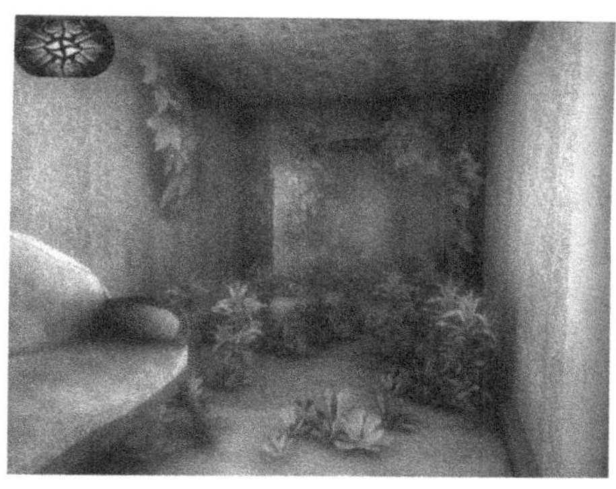

Dementia

expected shadowy corners and hidden secrets expected of the haunted mansion horror subgenre, most people engaging with the game will doubtless be subconsciously anticipating particular shocks to play out in specific ways, and thus it is much to the designers' credit that this expectation is actually only rarely met.

The developers make particularly good use of the capabilities of the Android operating system, combining impressive graphics (rendered with the Unity3D engine) with a touch-screen control system which makes movement and visual orientation seem almost counterintuitive until the player gets used to the process. Though it seems in stark contrast to the straightforward mouse-driven system of interaction utilised in similar games such as *RealMyst* (2000) or *Uru* (2003), these touch-screen control issues actually add to the game's general sense of disorientation (inadvertently or otherwise), as the initially unreliable control over first-person navigation contributes a further degree of confusion to an already unfamiliar playing environment.

Delirium is also fairly swiftly introduced as an issue for the protagonist to confront throughout the game, primarily in the form of indistinct, chattering voices (the sound design is commendably atmospheric) and through the appearance of various visual anomalies which stem from – for instance – highly patterned wallpaper, which comes to seem as though it is something else entirely, occasionally even behaving like a living organism. To explain in greater detail would be to risk spoiling the deeply ambiguous secret which lies at the heart of the game, but suffice it to say that the judiciously-considered fusion of supernatural phenomena and impaired psychological perception remains significant throughout the game as it builds towards a dark and unforeseen climax.

Naturally there may well be some degree of debate over whether a horror narrative is necessarily the most appropriate setting for an exploration of dementia and its symptoms. Some will inevitably claim that such a scenario runs the risk of embellishing the condition's effects solely for dramatic purposes, somehow squandering the potential for a greater exploration of how dementia affects human senses in daily life. However, an important part of a condition becoming more widely accepted in popular culture is that it may inevitably find itself becoming applied in new configurations as its attributes are more fully explored by differing creative approaches. The horror scenario of *Dementia* may be an unfamiliar situation in which to encounter the consideration of mental illness within a gaming environment, but it is one which allows the designers to incorporate symptoms such as hallucinations and delirium in ways which make logical narrative sense given the nature of the storyline. For this reason alone, the artistic decision proves itself to be justifiable precisely because of its intention to explore the symptoms of dementia in a thoughtful and meaningfully-realised way, rather than simply including them for the purposes of employing the condition in an exaggerated or overdramatic manner simply to meet superficial ends.

With an obvious willingness to confront the effects of the condition head-on, *Dementia* was a brave attempt to explore the concerns and ramifications of mental health issues within an established gaming framework, thus presenting the unfamiliar using the apparatus of the recognisable and commonplace. Its attempts to combine psychic awareness with psychological disorientation, thus causing a clash between scientifically confirmed phenomena and empirically unprovable supernatural incidents, will doubtless seem contentious to many. And likewise, the use of hallucinatory imagery for the purposes of entertainment may not be to everyone's taste, no matter how meticulous or well-realised the strategy may be. However, with public enthusiasm for home virtual reality headsets now very much in vogue thanks to devices such as the Oculus Rift and Sony PlayStation VR headsets, as well as other similar hardware solutions designed to augment and redefine the playing experience in increasingly ground-breaking ways, games such *Dementia* may well prove to be ahead of their time. If its first-person depiction of dementia's effects can help to disseminate understanding of the condition and the nature of its symptoms amongst new audiences throughout the world, this provocative and challenging gaming experience may prove to be as timely as it was intellectually and emotionally enervating.

28
ILLUMINATION AND HALLUCINATIONS
Rainbird Software's Weird Dreams

ONE of the most demanding challenges facing emerging technologies in recent years has been the accurate simulation of hallucinations, a symptom of many forms of dementia and a phenomenon which causes often intense difficulty for people affected by the condition across the entire globe. While scientific apparatus has been able to simulate other effects of dementia – including problems with balance, visual acuity, and issues with the acoustic environment – the complex nature of hallucinatory experiences has made replicating the problem a time-consuming and thought-provoking trial for scientists and medical specialists alike. As virtual reality technology and other nascent software solutions are being developed with this goal in mind, however, it is important to remember that British computing talent was already engaging with the elaborate effort of depicting hallucinatory phenomena more than a quarter of a century ago.

Weird Dreams was one of the most distinctive – and unconventional – titles released in the era of the 16-bit computer. First released in 1989, the game was developed for the Atari ST and the IBM PC (a version for the venerable 8-bit Commodore 64 would be released a year later), but it is the graphically-impressive Commodore Amiga edition of the title that remains best-remembered. Coded by Herman Serrano for Rainbird Software (a videogame publisher which was a division of British Telecom), and featuring uniquely offbeat graphical design by Serrano and James Hutchby, *Weird Dreams* was nominally a flip-screen action adventure game... but as anyone who had ever played it would attest, no straightforward description could really do justice to the experience. Belonging to the cinematic platform action game genre, the colourful graphics and offbeat soundtrack of the Amiga version has lingered longest in the public consciousness, and the game became almost certainly the single most prominent depiction of mental health to have appeared on the computer during its glory years between the late 1980s and early 1990s.

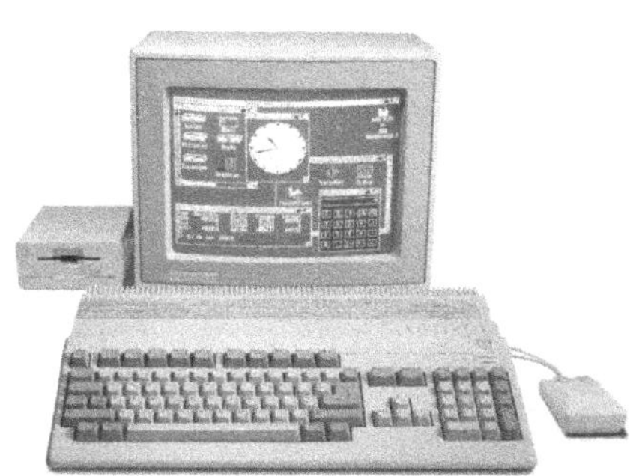

The Commodore Amiga 500

With a thriving public domain software scene and dedicated, innovative developers on both sides of the Atlantic, the Commodore Amiga was host to no shortage of inventive titles during its lifespan. The 16-bit boom was one of the most exciting periods in the history of early home computing, and the Amiga was very much at the forefront of this late eighties development due to its greatly advanced audio-visual capabilities, increased processor power, and superior amounts of memory compared to earlier 8-bit counterparts which dominated the earlier part of the decade. *Weird Dreams*, however, proved to be somewhat *avant-garde* even by the outré standards of this ground-breaking machine. The player takes the part of a patient who is undergoing neurological surgery, and finds their personal avatar (still clad in hospital pyjamas) cast adrift in a variety of seemingly innocuous situations which soon take a disturbing turn. The original release of the game was accompanied by a 64-page novella by author Rupert Goodwins, which recounted the rather convoluted story behind the medical difficulties affecting the protagonist. This explanatory narrative was not necessary to understand the game's action; however, like several other releases at the time, the booklet acted as a copy-protection device, as users had to input a random word when prompted to access the game, lessening the chances of software piracy.

As the game's title suggests, the action almost immediately becomes nightmarish as the central character encounters a range of commonplace locations and objects which – due to the hallucinatory effects that are affecting his perception – appear frightening or even deadly. During a walk in a peaceful country garden, an apparently-harmless bed of roses transpires to be a lethal hazard when the flowers grow teeth and start snapping uncontrollably, while a simple rotary lawnmower becomes a life-threatening menace which follows the player intimidatingly throughout the level, its jagged blades spinning like the prongs of a circular saw. Other stages of the game introduce a common wasp grown to Herculean proportions, clouds resembling flying fish (which can be plucked from the sky and used as a weapon), ordinary hallway doors which can tear the player in half, and many other seemingly-mundane items which have taken on a newly-dangerous form. But, the audience are asked to consider, are any of these situations truly what they seem to be?

The game becomes increasingly surreal as it progresses, its style suggesting Salvador Dali by way of Heath Robinson, leading to a climactic battle between the player and a gigantic cerebral cortex which signifies the fundamental struggle between reality and illusion. Yet even here, a successful outcome leads to an end-game sequence which raises almost as many questions as it answers. Supplanting the usual energy meters employed by more conformist gaming fare of the time is a simple heart rate monitor, which is agitated by encounters with the hallucinated phenomena and – if the beats per minute increase beyond a certain point – causes 'real-life' health problems for the player's character on the operating table, outside of their unconscious state. Accompanying the game is a hauntingly atmospheric score by legendary videogame composer David Whittaker, a recording artist who lent his talent to dozens of games throughout the eighties and nineties, which adds greatly to the ominous on-screen action.

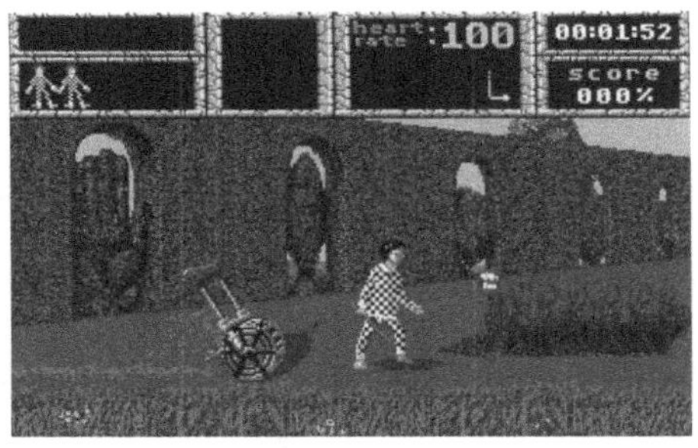

Weird Dreams

Although the game appears to toy with the human ability to differentiate between the perceptions of the conscious and unconscious mind (the closing sequence challenges us to ask whether the action we have witnessed has truly been a dream at all, thus querying the nature of 'true' reality), the designers' well-judged exploration of hallucinatory incidents was ultimately the reason why the game has continued to stand out after so many years. Though heavily criticised by the reviewers of the time for an extremely unforgiving difficulty level, where one wrong move can prove instantly fatal, the imaginative non-linear level design strategy and absurdist threats combined to make the game one of the most instantly memorable of the Amiga's early years.

Perhaps because of its sheer distinctiveness, *Weird Dreams* was a popular title, and conversions of the game were planned for the Sinclair ZX Spectrum, Amstrad CPC and BBC Micro (though none of these versions would ultimately materialise). Part of its appeal, aside from the considerable ingenuity of its central premise, has been the level of challenge that it presented the player. Though the degree of dexterity required to keep the protagonist alive was fairly high compared to other titles in the genre that were available at the time, it was the unpredictability of unfolding events which made gameplay particularly compelling. Though proceedings often made little rational sense, the game demonstrated a sort of ironclad internal logic all of its own, and trial and error was essential if the player was to discover a way to advance through the various demanding levels in the order of their choosing. Puzzles often had head-scratchingly obscure solutions, and with even the most innocuous items becoming dangerous threats in the blink of an eye, the game's point about the importance of reliable sensory perception could scarcely have been more immediate.

So what kind of lessons may be learned from *Weird Dreams* and its careful balance between unabashed surrealism and the lurking danger beneath the commonplace veneer of everyday situations? In its sinister use of absurdity and unremittingly dark tone, the game was to predate the boom in the psychological horror video-gaming genre by some years, anticipating far more popular international titles such as Capcom's *Resident Evil* cycle (1996–) and Konami's *Silent Hill* series (1999–). Yet its carefully considered and imaginatively-designed use of hallucinatory phenomena was to give the public a brief but provocative glimpse into the frightening effects that mental health conditions such as dementia may cause, laying the groundwork for explorations of such disorders which remain relevant in the present day. Here we witness the concept of hallucinations not in the form of mere entertainment within an action-based game, but rather as an examination of the boundary between the real and the imagined, the fragile line between conscious awareness and unconscious threat. And that, perhaps, is the true and lasting legacy of *Weird Dreams*: that by implementing such a framework through the seemingly-familiar guise of an action adventure game, the audience becomes more fully aware of the true extent of this existential anxiety as they are encouraged to perceive the underlying nature of the central dichotomy more fully than they may have done before.

29

INNER DISQUIET IN OUTER SPACE

Visceral Games's Dead Space

MODERN computer gaming has served up no shortage of entries in the increasingly well-populated genre of the first-person shooter, and among the more inventive experiments to arrive in the field in recent years has been Visceral Games' atmospheric *Dead Space* trilogy (2008-13), a popular series of survival horror adventures situated in futuristic science fiction locales. Appearing on the Sony PlayStation 3 and Microsoft Xbox 360, as well as on Windows PCs, the *Dead Space* cycle has spawned a multimedia universe which has thus far included comic books, mobile gaming apps, animated films, and prose novels.

The trilogy's protagonist, Isaac Clarke, may well have been named in recognition of two pioneering giants from the annals of literary sci-fi, but the cerebral work of Isaac Asimov or Arthur C. Clarke never reached the uncompromisingly dark or gruesome depths of *Dead Space*. Yet although the cycle's claustrophobic environment and copious macabre gore (a highly effective melange of the Lovecraftian uncanny and Cronenbergian body horror) have won it many admirers amongst the critical community, perhaps the most remarkable – and somewhat unexpected – innovation of the *Dead Space* games has been its ground-breaking depiction of dementia.

Dementia in *Dead Space* is not the result of the progression of a particular psychiatric condition; rather, the disorder occurs due to the malign influence of ancient alien artefacts called Markers. When excavated in the 25th century, these Markers have various unpredictable effects on the different characters of the game, including the player-controlled protagonist. Symptoms may include delusions and vivid hallucinations, abrupt changes in personality (including acute paranoia), hysteria, and unanticipated impediments to reasoning – all of which can have potentially lethal consequences in an inhospitable environment filled with deadly, mutated alien beings. The games' cleverly-designed, non-linear structure adds a further disjointed feel to proceedings.

The games' engagement with dementia is far from superficial; rather, the condition drives the plot in interesting and unexpected ways. Characters who do not actually exist, or who have been dead for some time, appear to communicate with members of the trilogy's cast even though they are not actually present – a direct result of the Markers' potent capacity to induce delusion.

Because the player's character and the supporting *dramatis personae* are each affected in different ways by dementia, distrust regarding their various motivations (that is, the extent to which their perceptions may be considered reliable) runs rampant throughout the games in the cycle. The unfamiliarity of the series' far-flung locales, which include abandoned mining vessels, expansive space stations, and desolate ice worlds, only increases the sense of apprehension and general unease – not least when traversing dimly-lit areas in zero gravity or racing to conserve rapidly-diminishing oxygen supplies in the cold vacuum of space.

Further heightening the stakes of the game is the fact that so many of the difficulties encountered throughout the narrative (the majority of them being life-threatening in one way or another) require manual dexterity and problem-solving skills. Because the symptoms of dementia, as they are presented within the game, have the capacity to violently disrupt the player's abilities, major challenges can be encountered at the least expected moments. Clarke, an engineer, must rely upon his improvisational skills to devise technical solutions, and – with a volatile grip on his perception – danger can lurk around just about any corner: especially given the presence of hazardous environment conditions, zero gravity areas, and of course the dogged pursuit of the game's antagonists, the mutated, zombie-like Necromorphs.

While there is little doubt that *Dead Space* owes much of its horror content to its grisly alien adversaries (actually the reanimated corpses of human beings, now under the control of an alien parasitic organism), the ensuing carnage and blood-soaked dismemberment is only one factor of what makes the cycle such a disquieting experience. As interactive narratives go, *Dead Space* is so much more than simply a survival movie set in dark, far-flung corners of the cosmos. Though occasional visual callbacks to influential sci-fi films such as John Carpenter's *The Thing* (1982) and James Cameron's *Aliens* (1986) are undeniable, the games very much forge their own path, and the many unanticipated twists and turns throughout the plot (and indeed from one entry in the series to the next) provides gameplay with plenty of genuine surprises. However, what truly separates the *Dead Space* series from its many competitors is the way in which the continual threat of disruption to the central character's senses can add an additional layer of jeopardy to the action at any time.

Altered states of being were not new to the first-person shooter, with Valve Corporation's sublime *Half-Life* (1998) and its ground-breaking sequel *Half-Life 2* (2004), along with their numerous expansions, dealing with alternate dimensional realities and systems of matter teleportation which regularly went awry. These innovations, however, were all related to external phenomena; although familiar Earth-based settings gradually became more and more alien and threatening due to extra-terrestrial (and extra-dimensional) incursions, the games' protagonist Dr Gordon Freeman generally found that his own sensory perspective on events remained reliable throughout the games' events. The action of *Dead*

Space differed, however, in the sense that Isaac Clarke not only found himself unable to trust his surroundings – where the mundane could very quickly transform into the lethally-destructive at a moment's notice – but also that his awareness and discernment of events was similarly tenuous and potentially precarious. Naturally this meant that situations which had mission-altering consequences could transpire to be entirely illusory, or that a straightforward task suddenly becomes difficult or even impossible due to the deterioration of motor skills or observational ability. In addition to the treacherous environments presented by the games – all of them extreme in one way or another – there was an indisputable sense of perpetual danger surrounding the playing experience which truly did set the games apart from many other interactive sci-fi action adventures.

Given its developer's stated aim to present the most frightening game possible with the technology available at the time, there was no doubting the fact that *Dead Space* and its sequels were all superbly geared to provide their fair share of shocks. The games' sound design in particular was superb, delivering creepily atmospheric environments where the ominous sound of deadly threats always seemed to be mere moments away. Highly polished, and continually refined with each successive entry in the series, Visceral Games produced a survival horror experience which established itself as one of the leading intellectual properties in the genre at the time. Yet for all the complex and involving plotlines which run throughout the main trilogy, gameplay would not have seemed nearly so discomfiting if Clarke had been in full command of his senses throughout. With the threat of intense delirium always hovering over events, players could never be quite sure if their strategies could be enacted without a sudden lurch in their character's manual abilities or powers of perception. It was arguably his development, even more than the innovative mutant enemies which came to popularise the trilogy in gaming culture, which made these titles so memorable.

Dead Space is a series which has succeeded admirably in the evocation of peril, ratcheting up one hazardous situation after another as it skilfully shreds the nerves of the player. In these games, dementia may be a condition which makes the protagonist – and the person controlling him – doubt their responses and distrust their own impulses at every turn, but it also proves itself to be an adversary which is every bit as dangerous as the deadly Necromorphs which implacably hunt their prey throughout the events of the cycle. But somehow, Visceral Games managed to avoid sensationalising either the disorder or its place in the game. While *Dead Space* acknowledges the many practical difficulties that the condition can present, it also views them through the lens of an extreme environment which would be risk-laden even at the best of times, heightening the general sense of risk and vulnerability facing the protagonist. And while many clinical psychiatrists would no doubt be quick to observe that many of the symptoms in the game are presented in a particular manner that would likely prove rare and/or more intense in their depiction than would be encountered in a majority of real-life forms of dementia, if the *Dead Space* cycle succeeds (even inadvertently) in raising general awareness of the complications and anxieties inherent in the disorder then it has achieved much more than providing a hyper-realistic and intricately-plotted slice of sci-fi horror for home gaming consoles.

30

VIRTUAL WORLDS AND MINDSCAPES

White Paper Games's Ether One

DELVING into the intricate depths of the human psyche may seem an unlikely strategy to form the basis of an entertaining video game, but in actuality this very concept has been at the heart of some of the most memorable gaming experiences of recent years. The approach has been particularly notable in Ubisoft's massively successful *Assassin's Creed* series (2007-), where febrile recollection and uncertain personal experiences collide to produce vivid abstract landscapes as a result of the Animus, the games' fictional technological interface which allows the user access to the subconscious memories of the protagonist's ancestors over centuries past. However, it has only been since the turn of the decade that dementia has truly been given the chance to explicitly take centre stage as the subject of computer entertainment, and few examples of this kind of game have captured the imagination quite as comprehensively as White Paper Games's *Ether One*.

Released in March 2014 for Windows-based PCs, with a PlayStation 4 conversion being launched the following year, *Ether One* immediately caught the imagination of commentators, including many beyond the confines of the computer gaming community. Publications as diverse as *The New Yorker* and *Popular Mechanics* praised the title for its sensitive, non-exploitative exploration of the psychological effects of dementia, and the inventive way in which White Paper Games – an independent British software house – achieved their creative aims. The company had been little heard of prior to the release of this, their debut title, but its success made certain that they would soon be established as a force to be reckoned with in the graphic adventure genre.

Using a first-person perspective, the game places the player in the role of a technician in the employ of the Ether Institute of Telepathic Medicine – an operative who is using a complex virtual reality system to explore the memories of an individual who has been diagnosed with dementia. During this search around the mind of the person in question, the effects of the disorder soon become apparent – missing memories must be reconstructed and reclaimed, the process of restoration taking the form of logic puzzles and other symbolically constructive strategies.

The gaming experience is, of course, rather more complex than the above summary suggests, and the player quickly finds themselves cast adrift in the enigmatic settlement of Pinwheel, an metaphoric interpretation of a mind undergoing changes wrought by dementia in strange and often unpredictable ways. There are a handful of different environments for the player to explore, and from each they must collect a series of red ribbons (for reasons which eventually become clear). An ominous sense of unease – sometimes intriguingly mystifying, at other times oppressively anxious – permeates the gameplay at times, with inscrutability lying very much at the heart of interaction with the gaming experience. The developers appeared to be acutely aware of the need for respect and empathy given the nature of the game's subject matter, and even critics who were sceptical of the notion that dementia would ever be a suitable focus for electronic entertainment would find difficulty in passing harsh judgment on the perceptive and thought-provoking approach which was taken. The player is left in no doubt that dementia is anything but a game, of course, but its treatment is undeniably a challenge and a puzzle for those who aim to cure the condition; it is this juxtaposition of compassionate understanding and analytical problem-solving which forms the bedrock upon which the game's objectives are founded.

With its highly distinctive, deliberately unsettling imagery and varied range of almost dreamlike experiences, *Ether One* is something of a design triumph. In its subtle subversion of the everyday and mundane into the naggingly disconcerting, the game recalls other titans of the first-person perspective adventure/exploration narrative such as Davey Wreden's *The Stanley Parable* (2011) the Fullbright Company's *Gone Home* (2013) – thought-provoking titles which contrasted the recognisable with the forebodingly unfamiliar to highly successful effect. There is much to admire about the way that the immersive but bizarre nature of the game world evokes the off-kilter physical dynamics of titles such as the Valve Corporation's acclaimed *Portal* (2007), for instance, while the prominent lighthouse and old-fashioned gears and analogue dials seem like an obvious tip of the hat to Cyan Worlds's *Myst* (1993), the pioneering giant of the first-person puzzle/mystery game which was to kick-start the genre at the advent of the CD-ROM drive revolution back in the early nineties. Yet in truth, *Ether One* does not seek to impose the abstruse complexity so often found in the cerebral brainteasers of *Myst* or its numerous sequels (including *Riven*, 1997, and *Exile*, 2001), any more than it allows its qualities of exploration and self-discovery to overshadow the sense of disorientation and ambiguity which lies at the game's heart.

As might be expected from a title that was in development for three years, the final product is a glossy and accomplished gaming experience. Though *Ether One* can be completed in as little as five hours' worth of gameplay, this would be to overlook the temptation to spend time exploring the unique environment that is presented and soak in its distinctive ambience. The game's puzzles can vary from physical tasks through to mental conundrums, but their level of difficulty gradually increases as the story continues. The narrative also contains a significant twist in that the protagonist, who is presumed to be an outside operative aiding in the treatment of a person with dementia, actually transpires to be rather more closely associated (and psychologically invested) in the task at hand than is immediately obvious at the beginning of the game.

A simple but powerful system of symbolism is established throughout the events of *Ether One*, which inclines the exploration of this seemingly abstract, arbitrary environment towards a range of more concrete objectives. Impaired memories are represented by broken reel-to-reel projectors, while the dementia itself is signified by gemstones which can be destroyed by 'the artefact'; a hand-held lamp with initially-unexplained properties. While Pinwheel may at first seem like a random or somehow figurative location for the game's events, its significance is eventually detailed – a revelation which has major implications for the game's characters as their identities and relationships are slowly fleshed out and elaborated upon.

Reviewers of *Ether One* were largely complimentary about White Paper Games's depiction of dementia, praising the way in which the title charts cognitive decline without simply turning the symptoms of the condition into a plot device. While combating dementia is at the core of the game, puzzle-solving is necessary not only to hold back the progression of the disorder, but also to piece together the history behind the person who is affected by it. This inevitably places the onus on the player to chart the various fragments of evidence that they are able to collect along their journey as they slowly construct a meaningful history of events and try to establish their character's role in the plot. The eventual revelation, when it comes, will be a genuine surprise to many, and the game encourages emotional investment in its central figures just as much as it stimulates curiosity to encourage players into uncovering as many hidden mysteries as possible. There is a sense of nostalgic melancholy throughout proceedings – between the bygone landscapes of old, depopulated (but distinctively British) settings and N.J. Apostol's wistful, minimalist original score for the game – which corresponds to the action in highly effective ways. Yet for all the game's sophisticated contrast of the impeccably detailed and the enigmatically abstract, there is no doubting the fact that dementia is placed front and centre in the gameplay experience. With its mirroring of the symptoms of dementia in the splintered, non-linear storytelling and frequently jarring clash between the comfortingly familiar and starkly alien, players could experience cognitive deterioration and failure of memory much more explicitly than had been the case in other video-gaming titles prior to this point.

With a narrative that raises almost as many questions as it answers, and an emotionally affecting conclusion which divided the opinions of reviewers at the time of its release, *Ether One* proved to be a breath of fresh air in a gaming world that was increasingly dominated by big-name franchises. While the point-and-click adventure game has experienced something of a renaissance in recent years, especially with increased access to such titles on mobile platforms, the White Paper Games development team created a gameplay experience that stood apart even in the resourceful and creatively fertile world of independent videogame studios. Perhaps more prominently than in any other game to date, the player witnesses dementia being depicted in a wide variety of different ways – as the pursuit of meaning, a puzzle to be solved, and a lost history to be restored. Allegory abounds as seemingly disparate objects are collected for unknown future purposes, broken machinery is repaired, numeric codes are entered, and – bit by bit – shattered memories are painstakingly reconstructed in unforeseen ways. *Ether One* may be a singularly unique take on mental illness, but it is one which proves distinctive enough to remain in the player's recollection long after its closing scenes have played out.

31

MYSTERY AND SUSPENSE IN UNEXPECTED PLACES

Campo Santo's Firewatch

WHILE games involving dementia still remain relatively few and far between, titles which feature people who care for someone affected by the disorder have been even rarer. Yet the impact of looking after a loved one who has been diagnosed with dementia was to form a central thread of the story in Campo Santo's first-person graphic adventure game *Firewatch* – an unconventional premise which won it no small amount of praise at the time of its release.

Published in 2016 for desktop PC operating systems including Microsoft Windows, Apple OS X and Linux, *Firewatch* was later converted to various popular games consoles including the Xbox One, Sony PlayStation 4, and Nintendo Switch. Under the direction of Olly Moss and Sean Vanaman, and produced by Jane Ng and Gabe McGill, the game was released by

Campo Santo – an independent software developer founded in Washington State – in partnership with Oregon-based videogame publisher Panic. In less than a year, *Firewatch* had sold over a million copies, and went on to earn numerous awards including Best Indie Game at the Golden Joystick Awards 2016, Best Debut Game at the British Academy Games Awards in 2017, and Best Narrative at the Game Developers Choice Awards in 2017. At time of writing, across all platforms the game has sold in excess of two and a half million copies.

The game surrounds the experiences of a man named Henry (voiced by Rich Sommer), who is recruited as a fire lookout at Wyoming's Shoshone National Forest in 1989, following the devastation of the infamous wildfires at Yellowstone National Park the previous year. Henry applies for the job after his wife develops early onset dementia in her late thirties; as her symptoms progress rapidly, he becomes unable to cope on his own, and eventually her growing needs are cared for by her family who live in Australia. Seeking solace away from the obligations and accountabilities of his personal life, Henry pursues a new calling and eventually finds himself assigned to a firewatch – a lookout post within the forest, from where staff can spot any early sign of wildfires.

Much of the game centres around an exploration of Henry's character as it is expounded through his interactions with his supervisor, Delilah (voiced by Cissy Jones), via walkie-talkies. Delilah is based at another firewatch elsewhere in the forest, and her relationship with Henry is built up entirely through choices of dialogue – whether the player decides to respond in one particular way or another, or even elects to ignore Delilah's questions altogether. On his first day on the job, Henry is called to investigate a group of inebriated teens who are letting off fireworks near a lake (an illegal act, given the very real danger of accidentally starting an out-of-control fire in the forest), but returns to find that his watchtower has been ransacked in his absence. Hidden secrets and extraordinary revelations are soon encountered as Henry tries to uncover the truth behind what happened to his firewatch – an unfolding enigma which will rapidly become very personal both for Delilah and himself.

While graphic adventures featuring a first-person perspective and choice-related narrative outcomes can be traced back to the genre's glory days in the early nineties, including ground-breaking titles such as Trilobyte's *The 7th Guest* (1993) and Activision/Infocom's *Return to Zork* (1993), in execution the level of character-defining decisions throughout *Firewatch* probably feels closer in a way to the *Mass Effect* series (2007-12), BioWare's inventive trilogy of sci-fi role-playing games. While the outer space settings of the *Mass Effect* universe could not have been further removed from the naturalistic environments of *Firewatch*, BioWare's games were deeply concerned with moral choice and character development, with almost every decision made by the player having consequences of one kind or another – not just within individual games of the series, but between one entry in the cycle and another. While choices in the *Mass Effect* titles could eventually turn out to have galaxy-spanning ramifications, the decisions made by players in *Firewatch* were more intimate but no less significant – the difference was the extent to which they came to define the central relationship between the protagonist, Henry, and his supervisor Delilah. These interactions come to define the overall direction of the game, as well as building (or eroding) trust and a sense of interdependence between the pair. But just as significantly, their conversations help to give substance to Henry's character, elaborating on how he feels about his life and the choices he has made.

Firewatch should be commended for the understated way in which it deals with dementia. Henry's emotions regarding his wife's condition are subtly realised, and – though the issue is rarely the focus of the game's interactions – it is clear that the situation weighs heavily upon the character's mind. While the issue of caring for someone with mental health problems is only seldom addressed in videogames, the refined way in which the subject is tackled proves to be laudable precisely because of its understatement. Because the game focuses almost entirely on Henry's point of view, the only way that presents itself to explore his interpersonal relationships is through the aspects of his character that emerge through the available dialogue choices; an inspired and carefully selected range of discourse from writers Chris Remo, Jake Rodkin, Olly Moss, and Sean Vanaman.

The game's time period is also adeptly chosen by the developers; by setting the game in the late eighties and forcing the central character to rely on analogue tools such as a walkie-talkie, fold-out map, and magnetic compass, the playing experience is not simply lent a great deal of atmosphere, but also deftly sidesteps the fact that the presence of modern-day technology such as GPS tracking and smartphones would have completely changed the complexion of the game's predominant suspense elements. Critics praised the stylised artwork, sound design, original music, and most especially the voice acting for its evocation of a very specific time and place. While the sense of mounting tension is very effectively realised, however, the opinion of commentators was split with regard to the game's ultimate resolution, with its narrative effectiveness the subject of considerable debate.

Firewatch is an unabashedly adult gaming experience, as it never shrinks from its fundamental exploration of the ways in which individuals deal – by different means – with life-changing issues such as sickness and disease, personal misfortune and heartbreak, and even love and death. The developers know that we all have our own particular coping mechanisms for these issues, and so it is with the characters in the game; their problems are contended with through a mixture of stoic professionalism, grim humour, and the occasional glimpse of anxiety and alarm. Key to the game's ethos is the various characters' search for isolation: Henry, who is seeking to separate himself from the pain of having to deal with his wife's condition; Delilah, who it becomes clear is regretting specific decisions of her own; and other characters who are encountered along the way, whose desire to cut themselves off from society eventually leads to tragic consequences.

While the core relationship between Henry and Delilah has been the standout aspect that has helped the title to gain a stalwart following amongst gamers – and one of many reasons why it has come to earn so many industry accolades – there is more to *Firewatch* than the fact that the player holds so much sway in developing the rapport and personal connection between the protagonist and the lead non-player character. Though exploration and investigation are of central importance throughout the game, the crucial gameplay element is actually one of self-discovery; solving the mystery is as much a question of uncovering the reasoning behind Henry's own outlook and responses when the character is so clearly conflicted between a desire to do his job well on one hand, and just wanting to be left alone on the other. What makes the journey so personal is not simply the fact that the rarefied, uninhabited environment of rural Wyoming makes the focus on Henry seem so sharp, but also the fact that when the identity of the mysterious figure who has haunted the ill-starred protagonist is finally revealed, his motivation feels strangely logical precisely because of the way that it mirrors (in a similarly tragic way) the lead character's own desire for isolation from the outside world. In some ways, this sense of loneliness and seclusion echoed other popular graphic adventure titles of the time, such as The Chinese Room/SCE Santa Monica Studios' *Everybody's Gone to the Rapture*

(2016) and Giant Sparrow's *What Remains of Edith Finch* (2017), which has further enhanced the reputation of *Firewatch* as a modern cult classic of the genre.

With its profound commentary on human vulnerability and the ways in which people sometimes feel compelled to retreat from their everyday lives when they feel unable to cope with them in an effective or constructive way, *Firewatch* was a remarkably mature gaming experience which, by its conclusion, left its protagonist with no hiding place. The title certainly exhibited an unconventional approach to dementia within a gaming experience, but – precisely because of this alternative methodology – the ramifications of dementia on those who care for someone with the condition was to feel all the more striking. And while, of course, the game was not to posit any comfortable solutions to life's problems, it did nonetheless highlight the importance of interpersonal relationships when it comes to getting through private difficulties. For although sharing a problem offers no guarantee that a resolution will be found more readily, it does suggest that support and realisation can sometimes be found in the least expected of places: a positive philosophy which has the ability to provide succour, and not just to people who find themselves taking up the responsibility of a caring role.

32 DIGITAL CHALLENGES WITH REAL-LIFE BENEFITS
Glitchers's Sea Hero Quest

ALMOST certainly the most widely-reported incidence in recent years of dementia in video-gaming has been *Sea Hero Quest*, an app for mobile devices which has captured the imagination of many commentators not because of the way in which its storyline showcases the condition, but rather on account of the tangible manner in which its players have aided dementia research. Released by software developer Glitchers in 2016, *Sea Hero Quest* is available for the Android and Apple iOS operating systems, and immediately found popularity amongst the gaming community.

The game began its life as the result of an initial premise by Professor Michael Hornberger, head of the department of applied dementia research at the University of East Anglia, who worked in collaboration with Dr Hugo Spiers and other neuroscientists from University

College London. The game was eventually designed and implemented by East London-based videogame developer Glitchers, in association with Alzheimer's Research UK and Deutsche Telekom. Glitchers had already established a firm reputation as a publisher of quirky and intelligently-written games such as pirate adventure *Plunderland* (2012) and management simulator *Chippy* (2013), amongst numerous others. However, *Sea Hero Quest* has rapidly become its most famous title to date, with the game having been downloaded on more than three and a half million occasions at time of writing.

Hornberger had previously collaborated with Glitchers on the well-received platform game *Find the King* (2015), in association with the Wellcome Trust. That title had explored the effects of the progression of dementia on its central character, a wizard who is in search of the kingdom's monarch. When one of the wizard's spells leads to unpredictable results, he must search the king's castle with the aid of various pages of his journal that are scattered around the rooms, and also cribbing clues from a range of mysterious handwritten notes. Throughout the game, the player must steer the wizard through disorientation and moments of confusion in order to achieve their objective, though the experience is not without a few shock revelations along the way.

Aside from the common theme of dementia, *Sea Hero Quest* could not have been more different from *Find the King*. The game's narrative is deceptively simple. The protagonist's father, a noted oceanographer, has spent his long career mapping waterways and encountering new sea life. However, now affected by dementia, he is unable to recall many of the details of the creatures he faced or the travels he had undertaken, and thus it is up to his offspring to take up the mantle and rediscover these findings for themselves. Thus the player must travel the seas in search of pages from the old oceanographer's journal, and with the objective of building a visual record of some of the unique marine life as he moves from one region to another. In the manner of many mobile titles, the game progresses from level to level and from stage to stage. Each section consists of a variety of different level styles, which include three-dimensional navigation (where the player is shown a paper map of the area and must visit a number of marker buoys in a specific order), an orientation test (where a flare gun must be aimed and fired at a particular site that is out of view, but which may lie in one of three specific directions), and a photographic challenge (where a snapshot of a sea creature must be taken at exactly the right point).

The game's touch-screen controls are intuitive and thus may be learnt quickly by the player, and the game's relaxed difficulty curve and polished presentation lend it an addictive quality which encourages 'just one more go' as the main character's ship advances through a range of environments including frozen conditions, a subtropical setting, and so forth. But the factor which drove players onward, more than any other aspect of the game, was the knowledge that every level they completed was genuinely helping to drive forward dementia research in the real world.

As was widely reported on television and in the press at the time of *Sea Hero Quest*'s release, the game had been designed with the specific purpose of charting players' mental acuity in relation to skills of three-dimensional navigation. As this particular ability tends to be adversely affected at an early stage in someone who has dementia, information regarding the nature and rate of its deterioration is of considerable interest to neuroscientists. When first run, the game requests a certain amount of anonymous demographic information from the player, such as their age, gender, and whether they are left-hand or right-hand dominant. (It is, however, not necessary to disclose these details in order to play the game.) The statistics supplied are then used along with data from the player's progress through the game in order to build up a picture of how spatial and directional ability is affected over time, taking into account facts such as how old each player is, their geographical location, and so forth. As the game has been played by literally millions of people in a total of 193 countries, it has generated 15,000 years' worth of dementia research data thus far, with several years of the project still to run.

The research which has been collected from the public is vastly in excess of what may otherwise have been amassed under laboratory conditions, and it is hoped that the information gathered will eventually facilitate the design of new diagnostic testing methods which will chart with greater accuracy when directional and spatial abilities are in decline. The statistics provided by players of *Sea Hero Quest* have aided researchers in compiling very comprehensive conclusions concerning whether navigational proficiency varies from country to country, how age affects the capacity to plot a route over time, and even less obvious factors such as whether the average amount of sleep a person gets per night has an effect on their spatial and/or directional capability.

Due to its combination of creditable scientific aims and being genuinely entertaining to play, *Sea Hero Quest* has not only proven to be popular with gamers – it has also been praised by critics and recognised by awards bodies, including the game winning nine Cannes Lion Awards at the International Festival of Creativity in 2016. A virtual reality version of the title, *Sea Hero Quest VR*, was released in 2017. While developed with the same ethos as the original game, the VR version allows even more detailed information to be added to the data set being collected by researchers, taking into account the co-ordination of head tilts and turns that can be detected using a virtual reality headset. Though the new game retains the checkpoint search and flare gun directional test from the original title, it also adds a new section – the Morris Water Maze – which facilitates the evaluation of spatial memory skills and learning abilities. Though *Sea Hero Quest VR* has not yet been as widely disseminated as the pioneering original, it has nonetheless achieved over 100,000 installations which have produced an amount of data comparable to 230 years' worth of research collated in a laboratory setting. The VR version of the game was conferred the Social Impact Award at the 2018 Webby Awards, as well as receiving a nomination in the Game Beyond Entertainment category at the British Academy Games Awards in 2018.

Sea Hero Quest has quickly become recognised as a global benchmark for data collection relevant to specific research needs; every level is painstakingly designed to ensure that the information collated from each player was pertinent to the researchers' needs. Yet in addition to its undeniable contribution to neuroscience, the game was also a triumph of public awareness, ensuring that dementia was firmly in the news across the world as the title's advantages were extolled by media outlets. Not only did the innovative qualities of the game appeal to people, but so did the altruistic sense that by donating their time to play a free game, members of the general public could add their own personal involvement to the fight against dementia. Someone who would never have considered signing up as a volunteer for medical testing in a laboratory might nevertheless be happy to spend a few minutes interacting with a mobile app, and as such they had helped to add the equivalent of several hours' worth of data to the information available to researchers. In this sense, the game and those behind it – scientists and software developers alike – have placed themselves at the cutting edge of an exciting and valuable new movement; one which has the capacity to transform the way that the public perceives participation in academic research.

Sea Hero Quest may seem like the culmination of a long and painstaking development process – one which has demonstrated, as its ultimate objective, many applications that have the potential to improve the lives of people with dementia. But of course, its success has proven that it has even greater significance. The title may well mark the beginning of an entirely new development in both game design and the public appreciation of science, ensuring that just as interactive entertainment has been firmly recognised as more than simply a casual diversion, so too is the stigma towards dementia and other mental health conditions being vigorously challenged by industry professionals across disciplines and throughout the world. For all those experts and specialists in their respective fields, labouring industriously to give a voice to people with dementia and to disseminate the subject in popular culture, the work continues. But today, as never before, the issue of dementia is finally being acknowledged as one which must be more frankly debated, more widely discussed, and more intently explored by the mainstream mass media if it is to be given the prominence in public discourse that it so clearly deserves.

Image Credits

Page 5: Image of Stephanie Cole by Hydealfred is licensed under the Creative Commons Attribution-Share Alike 3.0 Unported license [https://creativecommons.org/licenses/by-sa/3.0/]. Wikimedia Commons.

Page 28: Image of Alan Alda by Alan Kotok is licensed under the Creative Commons Attribution 2.0 Generic license [https://creativecommons.org/licenses/by/2.0/]. Wikimedia Commons.

Page 39: Image of Jonathan Frakes by Peter Chiapperino is is licensed under the Creative Commons Attribution 4.0 International license [https://creativecommons.org/licenses/by/4.0/]. Wikimedia Commons.

Page 42: Image of Robert Picardo by Jeff Hitchcock is licensed under the Creative Commons Attribution 2.0 Generic license [https://creativecommons.org/licenses/by/2.0/]. Wikimedia Commons.

Page 50: Image of André Dussollier by Georges Biard is licensed under the Creative Commons Attribution-Share Alike 3.0 Unported license [https://creativecommons.org/licenses/by-sa/3.0/]. Wikimedia Commons.

Page 56: Image of Chazz Palminteri by David Shankbone is licensed under the Creative Commons Attribution 3.0 Unported license [https://creativecommons.org/licenses/by/3.0/]. Wikimedia Commons.

Page 59: Image of Susan Sarandon by Incase is licensed under the Creative Commons Attribution 2.0 Generic license [https://creativecommons.org/licenses/by/2.0/]. Wikimedia Commons.

Page 66: Image of Trey Parker and Matt Stone by Ensceptico is licensed under the Creative Commons Attribution 2.0 Generic license [https://creativecommons.org/licenses/by/2.0/]. Wikimedia Commons.

Page 73: Image of David Mitchell and Robert Webb by Irving Liaw is licensed under the Creative Commons Attribution-Share Alike 2.0 Generic license [https://creativecommons.org/licenses/by-sa/2.0/]. Wikimedia Commons.

Page 84: Image of Ed Sheeran by Eva Rinaldiis is licensed under the Creative Commons Attribution-Share Alike 2.0 Generic license [https://creativecommons.org/licenses/by-sa/2.0/]. Wikimedia Commons.

Page 91: Image of Jill Sobule by Michael Borkson is licensed under the Creative Commons Attribution-Share Alike 2.0 Generic license [https://creativecommons.org/licenses/by-sa/2.0/]. Wikimedia Commons.

Page 116: Image of Whitechapel by MIKEDGAF714 is licensed under the Creative Commons Attribution-Share Alike 3.0 Unported license [https://creativecommons.org/licenses/by-sa/3.0/]. Wikimedia Commons.

Page 139: Image of Adam Young by _rockinfree is licensed under the Creative Commons Attribution 2.0 Generic license [https://creativecommons.org/licenses/by/2.0/]. Wikimedia Commons.

Page 158: Image of Sir Tom Courtenay by Siebbi is licensed under the Creative Commons Attribution-Share Alike 3.0 Unported license [https://creativecommons.org/licenses/by-sa/3.0/]. Wikimedia Commons.

Page 222: Image of the Sinclair ZX Spectrum by Bill Bertram is licensed under the Creative Commons Attribution-Share Alike 2.5 Generic license [https://creativecommons.org/licenses/by-sa/2.5/]. Wikimedia Commons.

Page 225: Screenshot from *iD* (CRL Software, 1986) on the Sinclair ZX Spectrum.

Page 232: Screenshot from *Dementia* (AGaming+, 2013) on the Android operating system.

Page 238: Image of the Commodore Amiga 500 by Bill Bertram is licensed under the Creative Commons Attribution-Share Alike 2.5 Generic license [https://creativecommons.org/licenses/by-sa/2.5/]. Wikimedia Commons.

Page 241: Screenshot from *Weird Dreams* (Rainbird Software, 1989) on the Commodore Amiga.

Acknowledgements

I am most grateful to my family, Julie Christie and Mary Melville, and to my friends Professor Roderick Watson, Amy Leitch, Eddy and Dorothy Bryan, Alex Tucker, Denham Hardwick MBE, David Addison, Ian McNeish, Dr Colin M. Barron, and Dr Elspeth King for their fellowship and encouragement throughout the course of this project.

About the Author

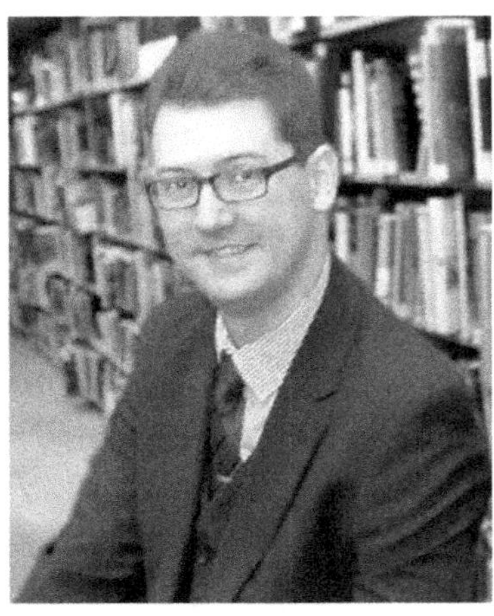

Dr Thomas Christie has many years of experience as a literary and publishing professional, working in collaboration with several companies including Cambridge Scholars Publishing, Crescent Moon Publishing and Robert Greene Publishing. A passionate advocate of the written word and literary arts, over the years he has worked to develop original writing for respected organisations such as the Stirling Smith Art Gallery and Museum and a leading independent higher education research unit based at the University of Stirling. Additionally, he is regularly involved in public speaking events and has delivered guest lectures and presentations about his work at many locations around the United Kingdom.

A member of the Royal Society of Literature, the Society of Authors, the Federation of Writers Scotland

and the Authors' Licensing and Collecting Society, he holds a first-class Honours degree in English Literature and a Masters degree in Humanities with British Cinema History from the Open University in Milton Keynes, and a Doctorate in Scottish Literature awarded by the University of Stirling.

He is the author of a number of books on the subject of modern film which include *Liv Tyler: Star in Ascendance* (2007), *The Cinema of Richard Linklater* (2008), *John Hughes and Eighties Cinema: Teenage Hopes and American Dreams* (2009), *Ferris Bueller's Day Off: Pocket Movie Guide* (2010), *The Christmas Movie Book* (2011), *The James Bond Movies of the 1980s* (2013), *Mel Brooks: Genius and Loving It!: Freedom and Liberation in the Cinema of Mel Brooks* (2015), and *A Righteously Awesome Eighties Christmas: Festive Cinema of the 1980s* (2016).

His other works include *Notional Identities: Ideology, Genre and National Identity in Popular Scottish Fiction Since the Seventies* (2013) and *The Spectrum of Adventure: A Brief History of Interactive Fiction on the Sinclair ZX Spectrum* (2016). He has also written a crowdfunded murder-mystery novel, *The Shadow in the Gallery* (2013), which is set during the nineteenth century in Stirling's historic Smith Art Gallery and Museum.

For more details about Tom and his work, please visit his website at:

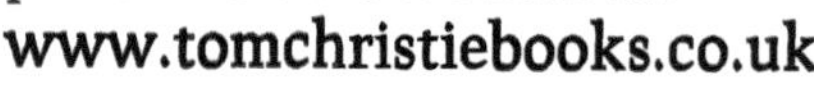
www.tomchristiebooks.co.uk

Also Available from Extremis Publishing

The Spectrum of Adventure

A Brief History of Interactive Fiction on the Sinclair ZX Spectrum

By Thomas A. Christie

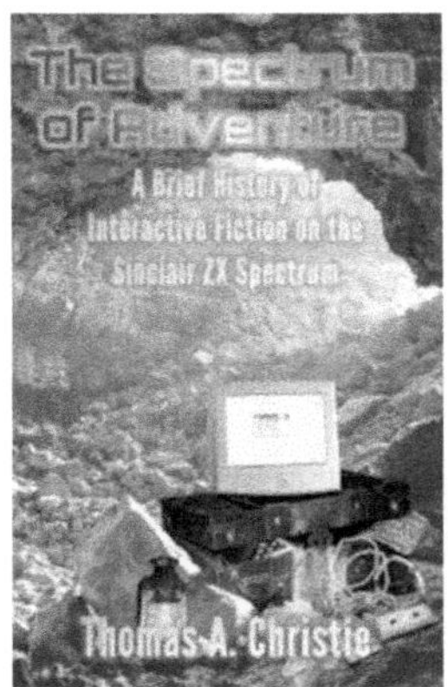

The Sinclair ZX Spectrum was one of the most popular home computers in British history, selling over five million units in its 1980s heyday. Amongst the thousands of games released for the Spectrum during its lifetime, the text adventure game was to emerge as one of the most significant genres on the system.

The Spectrum of Adventure chronicles the evolution of the text adventure on the ZX Spectrum, exploring the work of landmark software houses such as Melbourne House Software, Level 9 Computing, Delta 4 Software, the CRL Group, Magnetic Scrolls, and many others besides.

Covering one hundred individual games in all, this book celebrates the Spectrum's thriving interactive fiction scene of the eighties, chronicling the achievements of major publishers as well as independent developers from the machine's launch in 1982 until the end of the decade in 1989.

Also Available from Extremis Publishing

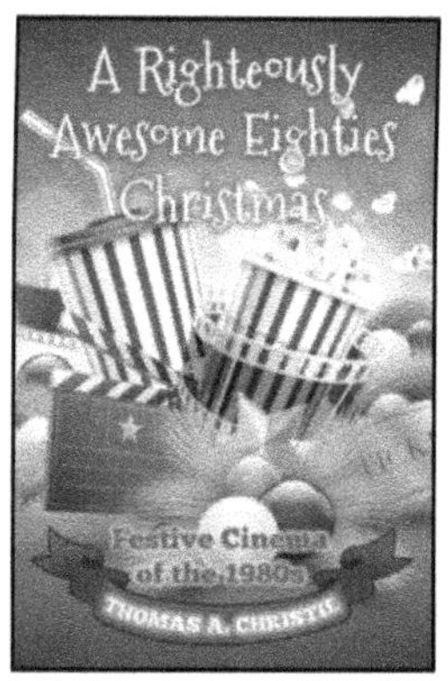

A Righteously Awesome Eighties Christmas

Festive Cinema of the 1980s

By Thomas A. Christie

The cinema of the festive season has blazed a trail through the world of film-making for more than a century, ranging from silent movies to the latest CGI features. From the author of *The Christmas Movie Book*, this new text explores the different narrative themes which emerged in the genre over the course of the 1980s, considering the developments which have helped to make the Christmas films of that decade amongst the most fascinating and engaging motion pictures in the history of festive movie production.

Released against the backdrop of a turbulent and rapidly-changing world, the Christmas films of the 1980s celebrated traditions and challenged assumptions in equal measure. With warm nostalgia colliding with aggressive modernity as never before, the eighties saw the movies of the holiday season being deconstructed and reconfigured to remain relevant in an age of cynicism and innovation.

Whether exploring comedy, drama, horror or fantasy, Christmas cinema has an unparalleled capacity to attract and inspire audiences. With a discussion ranging from the best-known titles to some of the most obscure, *A Righteously Awesome Eighties Christmas* examines the ways in which the Christmas motion pictures of the 1980s fit into the wider context of this captivating and ever-evolving genre.

Also Available from Extremis Publishing

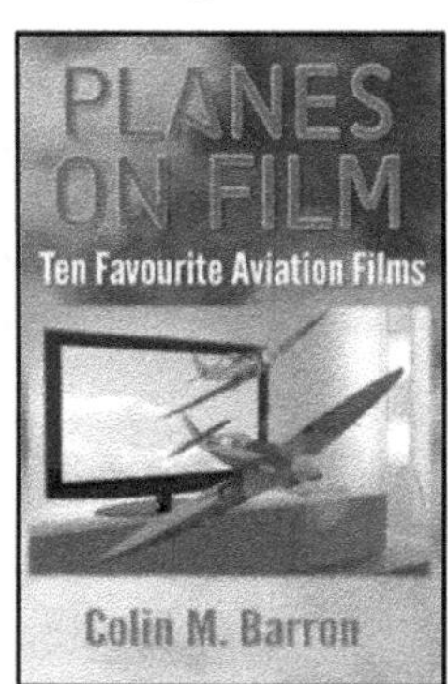

Planes on Film

Ten Favourite Aviation Films

By Colin M. Barron

One of the most durable genres in cinema, the aviation film has captivated audiences for decades with tales of heroism, bravery and overcoming seemingly insurmountable odds. Some of these movies have become national icons, achieving critical and commercial success when first released in cinemas and still attracting new audiences today.

In *Planes on Film: Ten Favourite Aviation Films*, Colin M. Barron reveals many little-known facts about the making of several aviation epics. Every movie is discussed in comprehensive detail, including a thorough analysis of the action and a complete listing of all the aircraft involved. With information about where the various planes were obtained from and their current location, the book also explores the subject of aviation films which were proposed but ultimately never saw the light of day.

With illustrations and meticulous factual commentary, *Planes on Film* is a book which will appeal to aviation enthusiasts, military historians and anyone who has an interest in cinema. Written by an author with a lifelong passion for aircraft and their depiction on the silver screen, *Planes on Film* presents a lively and thought-provoking discourse on a carefully-chosen selection of movies which have been drawn from right across the history of this fascinating cinematic genre.

Also Available from Extremis Publishing

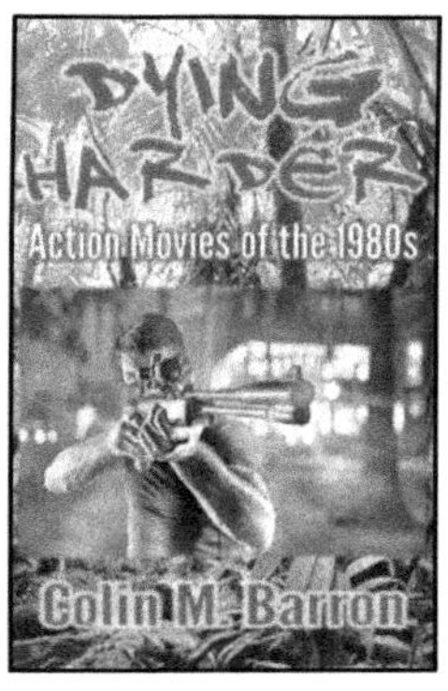

Dying Harder

Action Movies of the 1980s

By Colin M. Barron

The 1980s were a golden age for action movies, with the genre proving popular at the box-office as never before. Across the world, stars such as Sylvester Stallone, Arnold Schwarzenegger and Bruce Willis were becoming household names as a result of their appearances in some of the best-known films of the decade.

But what were the stories which lay behind the making of these movies? Why were the eighties to bear witness to so many truly iconic action features? And who were the people who brought these legends of action cinema to life?

In *Dying Harder: Action Movies of the 1980s*, Colin M. Barron considers some of the most unforgettable movies of the decade, exploring the reasons behind their success and assessing the extent of their enduring acclaim amongst audiences which continues into the present day.

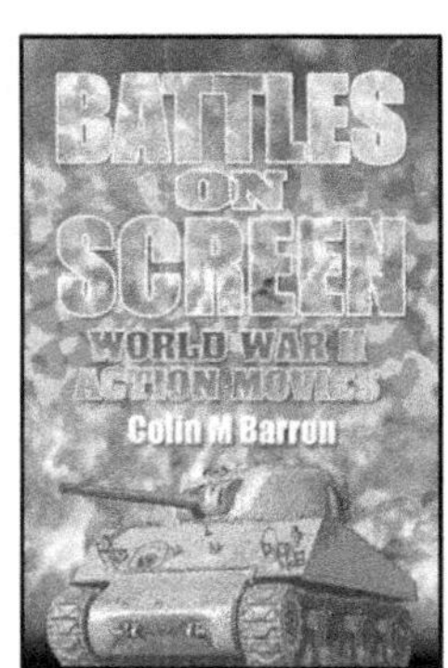

Battles on Screen

World War II Action Movies

By Colin M. Barron

The Second World War was one of the defining historical events of the Twentieth Century. This global conflict was responsible for enormous trials and great heroism, and the horrors and gallantry that it inspired has formed the basis of some of the most striking movies ever committed to celluloid.

From the author of *Planes on Film*, *Battles on Screen* offers both an analysis and celebration of cinema's engagement with World War II, discussing the actors, the locations, the vehicles and the production teams responsible for bringing these epics to life. Reaching across the decades, the impact and effectiveness of many classic war films are examined in detail, complete with full listings of their cast and crew.

Ranging from the real-life figures and historical events which lay behind many of these features to the behind-the-scenes challenges which confronted the film crews at the time of their production, *Battles on Screen* contains facts, statistics and critical commentary to satisfy even the most stalwart fan of the war movie genre.

Also Available from Extremis Publishing

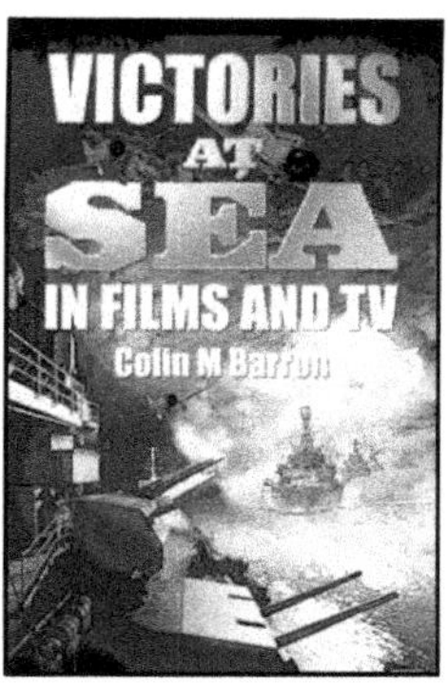

Victories at Sea

In Films and TV

By Colin M. Barron

Naval battles have inspired countless films and television dramas over the years, recounting the bravery and tragedy that have unfolded over centuries of conflict on the high seas. From the author of *Planes on Film* and *Battles on Screen*, this book examines some of the most exciting features that have dealt with naval warfare, exploring the ways in which they have achieved critical success and enduring popularity with audiences.

Victories at Sea considers the many different aspects of warfare on (and below) the waves as they have been depicted on screen, discussing such topics as amphibious operations, carrier warfare, underwater sabotage, and Cold War strategies. Covering films ranging from vintage World War II classics to modern seaborne thrillers, the book investigates the real-life stories which lay behind the production of these features as well as how they eventually came to be received at the box-office.

From blockbuster Hollywood epics to must-see television series, *Victories at Sea* is a comprehensive guide to the greats of the genre, combining a forensic eye for detail with meticulous analysis of the features under discussion. With discussion of low-budget dramas and high-octane action movies alike, this examination of naval warfare on the big and small screens relates all of the exhilaration and gallantry that have made these films such lasting favourites amongst cinema and TV aficionados.

For details of new and forthcoming books
from Extremis Publishing,
please visit our official website at:

www.extremispublishing.com

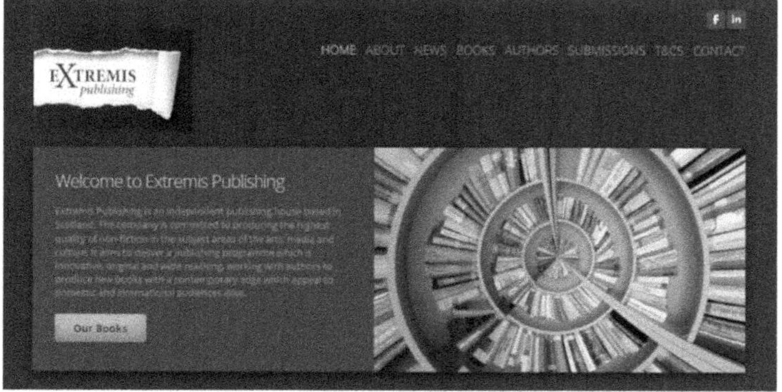

or follow us on social media at:

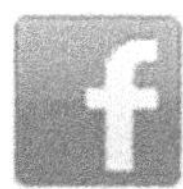

www.facebook.com/extremispublishing

www.linkedin.com/company/extremis-publishing-ltd-/

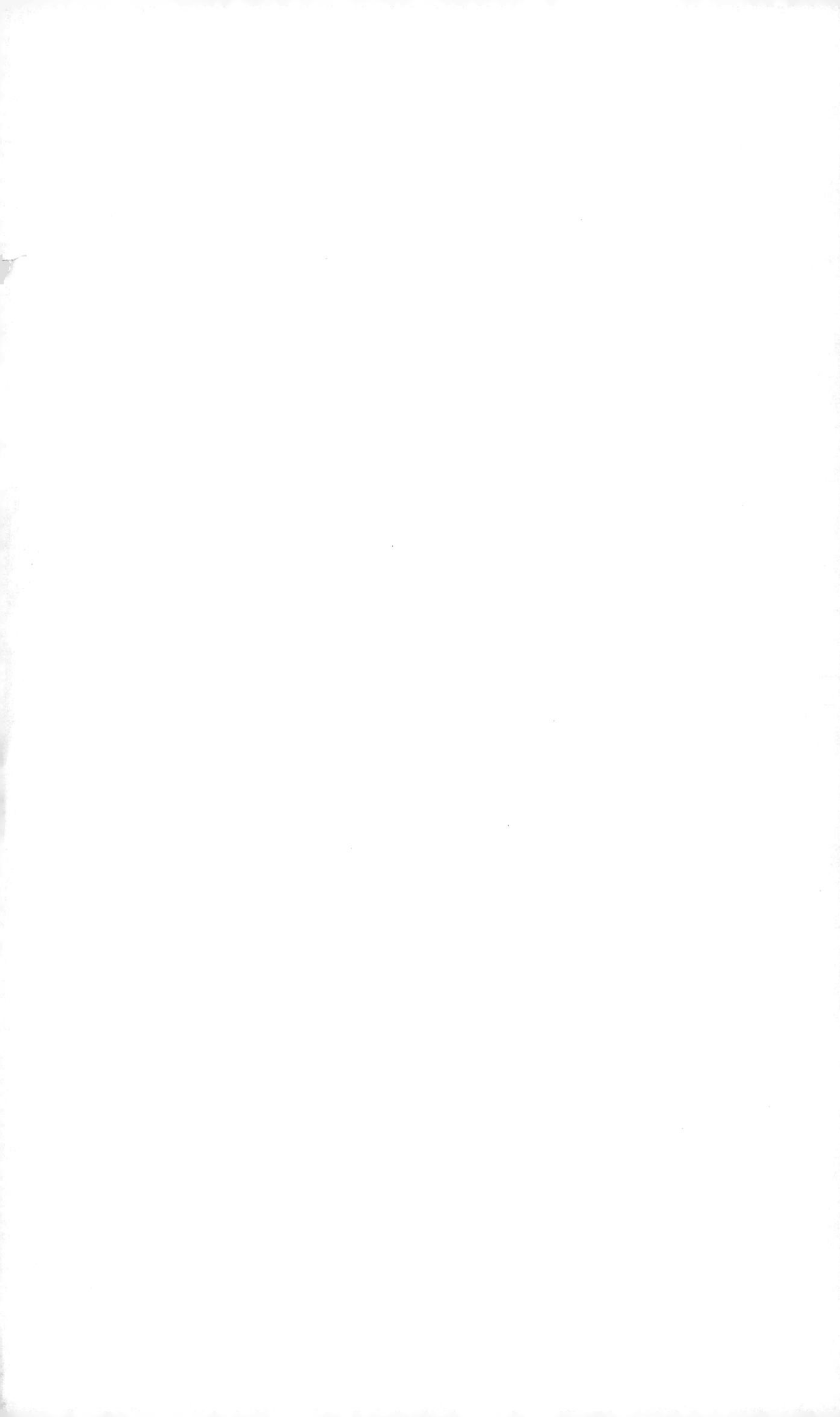

www.ingramcontent.com/pod-product-compliance
Ingram Content Group UK Ltd.
Pitfield, Milton Keynes, MK11 3LW, UK
UKHW020224250726
13967UKWH00001B/175

9 780995 589759